DOC EBONEE

The Courage to Trust

TIM O'NEAL

ROUND PEN PUBLISHING

Round Pen
PUBLISHING

Scripture references are from the New King James Version unless specified otherwise. (Nashville, TN: Thomas Nelson Publishers) Other versions and translations cited include:

New American Standard (NAS)

J.B. Phillips New Testament Translation (PHILLIPS)

ISBN #: 978-0-9908605-0-1

Cover Design: Diane Peterson, petersondesign@cox.net
Interior Graphic Design: Starr Clay, starrclay@comcast.net
Front Cover Photo: J Bar D Photography and Gordy Diers (P.O. Box 846, Delta, CO 81416)
Back Cover Photo: Toni O'Neal

TO

I would like to dedicate this book to those who have the courage to trust God's Word to change their thinking process, which will change their life.

Paul says in Romans 12:2 (PHILLIPS), "Don't let the world around you squeeze you into its own mold, but let God re-mold your minds from within, so that you may prove in practice that the plan of God for you is good, meets all his demands and moves towards the goal of true maturity."

The Testimonies that the Horses Can't Tell

This book is one of several books in a series titled The Testimonies that the Horses Can't Tell.

A testimony is a real-life story that conveys a memorable, transformative event. While a horse may not be able to *tell* its testimony, it certainly *displays* transformation—and renewed attitude and behavior—if a rider, trainer, or observer knows what to look for. Gypsy and Tim O'Neal know what to look for. And they know miracles when they see them!

Tim and Gypsy O'Neal each have decades of experience as horse trainers and more than fifty national and world championship titles in a variety of horse-show competitive classes involving quarter horses, pinto, palomino, and miniature breeds. The O'Neals know horses, and what it takes to train them, "show" them, and win!

Tim and Gypsy O'Neal are also deeply spiritual people with a great love for God's Word. They have been in active church ministry as pastors of a church in Kansas since 1998. In addition, both of them have spoken often in a variety of venues. Tim loves to preach "from the back of a horse," and many of his sermons are presented as illustrations of Bible truths at Cowboy Days and Cowboy

Weekends, horse shows, horsemanship clinics, and other events where people and horses come together in the context of faith and evangelism.

Through the years, the O'Neals have noted that horses can be exceedingly effective in helping people—especially in bringing them to emotional, psychological, and most importantly, spiritual healing. They have watched horses with certain characteristics—such as fear, depression, or anxiety—work with people who also struggled with these characteristics. The end result is often a horse that is healed, and a person who is healed. The processes of healing and overcoming are often parallel in the life of the horse and the life of the person working with the horse, with many of the same Bible-based principles involved.

Tim O'Neal has been quick to quote Will Rogers through the years: "The outside of a horse is good for the inside of a man."

You may order the books in this series from Tim O'Neal Ministries, P.O. Box 749, Fort Scott, Kansas 66701.

Books currently available in the series:

- *Doc Ebonee—The Courage to Trust*
- *Skeeter—Overcoming Fear*
- *Dandy—Victory over Bullies and Abusers*

Round Pen
PUBLISHING

CONTENTS

1

EAGER TO RIDE!

Doc Ebonee was exactly the horse I had been looking for.

He was a cutting horse with a little age on him, and significant show experience.

He was a money earner.

He had all the ingredients for fulfilling my ambition, which was to learn all he could teach me.

I was extremely pleased that our paths had crossed and he was about to be "my horse."

I could hardly wait to ride him.

And the day for that was very near! At least, in my opinion.

Two Important
Characteristics

As the story of Doc Ebonee unfolds, I believe it would be good for me to share with you at the outset two pieces of pertinent information. If you are familiar with the horse industry, you know these things. If you aren't, you might need to know these two things in order to fully appreciate Doc Ebonee's story, and how his story intersects with mine.

Horses are, by nature, anxious creatures. A key fact to remember in this story is that horses are fear-filled creatures, at least at the outset of a human-horse relationship. Most horses not only tend to shy away from strangers, but to *run* from strangers if they can. They are wary, keenly scrutinizing every move a person makes in their near presence. They are especially anxious if a stranger approaches them suddenly or with uneven movements, gestures, or loud sounds.

I usually use the term *anxious* rather than fear because fear is often linked to very specific incidents or memories. Anxiety is more pervasive—it is simply the "nature" of most horses. As such, anxiety is always a factor in training, even if a horse has been well cared for or trained in a gentle manner.

Why are horses anxious by nature? There are three main reasons, perhaps more:

One, for literally thousands of years, horses have been prey, not predators. They are herbivores, relying on grass and foliage for food, and if available, oats and other grains. They do not "hunt," but rather, are hunted by carnivores of all types as succulent, rather easily conquered prey.

Two, horses have virtually no self-defense system other than to run—and there are many predators who are faster. They can kick with their back legs, or rear up to come down on their front legs with a degree of power. Their teeth, however, are not of the "biting" kind as much as the "tearing" kind (they have a horizontal rather than vertical bite).

Because of their limited defensive ability, horses are *herd* animals. They find safety in numbers. In the wild, we see this often, and even horse-related animals, such as zebras, display this herd instinct. Horses that are suddenly in a one-on-one training environment with a human being are animals that have been stripped of their "herd." They have a double dose of anxiety—they are in a circumstance in which they suddenly are *not* in control and *cannot escape* and have *no companions* on which to rely for mutual safety.

There's certainly a good life sermon in that one fact alone—we human beings *also* do not do well when we are isolated from other human beings and find ourselves stripped of all ability to run away or defend ourselves in the face of perceived threat or danger.

If you pause to consider the number of people in our world today who live with a high level of anxiety, you'll probably come face to face with factors such as loneliness, a perceived lack of control, and an inability to escape a dangerous or uncertain situation. Human beings are anxiety prone, and so are horses.

Three, horses do not have visual depth perception. As a result, they are extremely wary of situations in which they cannot determine "how deep" something might be, either vertically or horizontally. They especially do not handle shadows or sources of water with confidence. A horse has no way of knowing if a puddle of water is a half-inch deep or twenty feet deep. It has no way of looking into a shadow, or determining if a dark cave is three yards deep or three hundred yards deep. This visual limitation only adds to the overall anxiety factor in most horses.

Again, we human beings aren't all that different. We tend to become increasingly *anxious* if we cannot determine precisely how a situation will turn out, or what might become of us in an unfamiliar circumstance with which we have no prior experience or training to handle.

All things taken together—the history of being "prey," a limited defensive ability, and lack of depth perception—it really is rather amazing that people have been able to tame and train horses! It truly is something of a miracle that *any* horse *ever* comes to trust a human being enough to act on the desire of that human being when it comes to crossing a creek or a river, jumping over a hurdle, or stepping into a deeply shaded area.

Horses have been bred through the years to display certain characteristics, or instincts. Most of the horses that compete at the top levels in show events are horses that have a fairly long ancestry of prizewinners as their pedigree.

Desirable "characteristics" are developed over generations of breeding. Certain instinctual traits of behavior, or muscular traits in conformation, are identified early in a horse and then are emphasized in training. As the desirable instinct or trait becomes more and more dominant, it also becomes more likely to be embedded in the DNA of the reproductive organs of the horse. The result, over time and generations, is eventually the development of very well-defined basic characteristics.

That is certainly the case with cutting horses.

The Unique Traits
of a Cutting Horse

A cutting horse is usually a very athletic and willing horse that possesses an innate "cow sense."

The cutting event in the show-horse world is an event in which a horse and rider are judged on their ability to separate a single animal away from a herd of cattle, and keep it away for a short period of time.

The sport originated on cattle ranches in the Old West of America, when it became a major job for a horse to separate cattle from a herd for the purposes of vaccinating, castrating, or sorting. Competitions naturally arose between the best horses and riders in a given area. The first cutting-horse competition was held in Texas in 1898, and over the years, a universal set of rules and regulations was developed. In 1946, the National Cutting Horse Association (NCHA) was founded.

The sport has grown rapidly through the years and there's a great deal of prize money associated with this event—more than $39 million dollars each year is awarded at NCHA-approved shows.

What Happens in This Event? A horse and rider select and separate a "cow" (usually a steer or heifer) out of a small herd of cattle, by moving between the cow and the herd. The separated cow will try to return to its herd. At that point the rider loosens the reins—in the horse world, we say "puts his hand down"—and leaves it entirely to the horse to keep the cow separated. The best horses love this job—they do it with savvy and style, and truly relish the task.

As a cow turns back toward its herd, the horse must draw back over its hocks and then turn with the cow. The rider is centered over the horse, keeping his or her eyes focused on the cow's head and neck in order to anticipate the cow's next move. The horse's shoulders during a run are parallel with that of the cow's. The horse and rider are judged on how the horse moves in relationship to the cow. Leg aids may be used to steady a horse and keep it from falling in on the cow or drifting toward the herd during a run.

Two riders are usually positioned on each side of the herd to help the cutter make his cut and to keep the herd grouped while the cutter works. These riders are called "herd holders." They help control the majority of the cattle so the rider can focus on a single cow that he is trying to separate from the herd. Two additional helpers, referred to as turnback men, help keep the separated cow in the working area stay turned back toward the exhibiting horse and rider. (They are like people in our lives who come along beside us to help us sort through the issues of life!)

A contestant has two and a half minutes to show the horse. Typically two or three cows are cut during a run. A judge awards points to the cutter using a scale that ranges from 60 to 80 points, with 70 considered average. The points are awarded or subtracted, as the competition is ongoing, with a final tally at the end of a run.

The rider needs to be aware of where he and his horse are within the defined competition area. If a rider and horse are out of position, they are penalized.

Points are awarded or subtracted for herd work, courage, eye appeal, controlling the cow, time worked, degree of difficulty, and loose reins.

The sport may initially seem complicated, but it is actually a fairly straightforward process and a great deal of *fun*!

Many of the events at horse shows are very quiet—there is tremendous concentration required by those who are showing, and the horses themselves. The cutting-horse class is different. It is more of an athletic event, and there is lots of whooping and hollering for both horses and riders, especially for horses that over time have become crowd favorites.

One of the interesting challenges for a person who wants to show or train for this event is to learn the jargon associated with the sport. If you go to a cutting-horse show, here are just a few of the terms you may hear among riders and judges:

- *Cheat:* a horse that looks for an easy way out of working correctly.
- *Collected:* a horse that is balanced under the rider so it can respond quickly to the moves of a cow.
- *Commit:* the intention to work a specific cow by looking at it and stepping toward it.
- *Deep cut:* picking a cow that is not at the edge of the herd. (Under NCHA rules, a cutter must make at least one deep cut into a herd.)
- *Draw cattle:* the horse's ability to make cows look at the horse and even move toward it.
- *Drop on a cow:* the crouching posture of the horse when a cow has been cut and separated, which usually occurs when the rider drops his rein hand on the horse's neck.
- *Dry work:* basic cutting-horse training done without the use of cattle. This is also called flatwork.

- *Heading a cow:* occurs when a rider places a horse in front of a cow in order to stop the cow or to force it to change directions.
- *Sweep:* when a horse sits back on its rear end and moves its front end, front legs extended, with a cow.

All of these things come clear when you are actually watching this event in competition, but I've provided that information here just for your amusement. The *sport* isn't complicated, but sometimes the terminology can seem complicated! That's like all of life, too, isn't it? We can get very bound up in words and their definitions, when most of behavior is far more black and white—at least from my perspective.

Before a run, a rider will usually watch other riders to see how the cattle are reacting and performing. In most cases, a rider will try to identify cows in advance that seem to be the easiest to separate. A cow selected by a rider needs to challenge but not overwhelm the horse.

A Range of Competitors. In the large horse shows, competition is usually available for riders in different divisions, for example:

- *Professional:* anyone who has received payment for training, riding, or showing in any equine discipline. (See amateur division below for the earnings level that qualifies a person as a professional.)

- *Non-professional:* a rider who does not train horses in any equine discipline—the horse must be fully owned by the non-professional, a spouse, or minor child.

- *Amateur:* a rider with lifetime earnings less than $50,000 in cutting competitions. An amateur may not work at a horse-training facility, nor be married to a professional trainer.

- *Youth:* riders who are eighteen years old or younger.

As the sport grows, other divisions are being added . . . frequently, it seems.

The Most Complicated Factor of All!

Now that you are well informed about cutting horses and the cutting-horse competitive world, we come to the most complicated aspect of training a horse and competing in the cutting events: the *rider*.

A rider needs to be so "in sync" with a cutting horse that the rider will know when to allow the horse to function according to its own instincts, and when to lead or guide the horse. In all other classifications of competition, the rider or trainer is fully in charge. The horse exists to perform at the rider's direction.

In the cutting classification, the horses have been bred for a "cow sense" that is *independent* of a rider's directions. The good cutting-horse rider is a person who knows when the horse is in "charge" and lets the horse move on its own.

Therein lies the challenge—especially for a rider who has grown accustomed to being in charge at all times!

I qualified as just such a rider.

Plus, when a rider is in a cutting-horse competition, there's a tremendous rush of adrenalin if the rider has a winning horse that really knows how to "cut" cattle.

I was a bit bored by the type of competing I had been doing up to that point in my life, and learning how to ride a cutting horse was a fun new challenge for me.

I could hardly wait!

2

BRINGING DOC EBONEE HOME

My wife Gypsy actually met Doc Ebonee before I did. We were not married at the time but had been dating for several months. On two different occasions in her life, Gypsy has found herself training horses that had a tremendous fear of *men*. They were just fine with her as a woman trainer and rider, but if you put those horses in the presence of men, they displayed a great deal of anxiety. Doc Ebonee turned out to be one of those horses.

When Gypsy entered Doc Ebonee's life, she was the first woman trainer he had known. She smelled different from a man, she treated him differently, and he responded to her differently! The minute he laid eyes on me . . . well, I was a *man*. And Doc Ebonee was at a place in his life where he no longer trusted men.

The first time I put a saddle on Doc Ebonee and led him out into the arena to ride him, I put my foot in the stirrup and started up, and he immediately darted away, taking my foot with him! If my foot had not been in the stirrup, I think he would have run as far away as possible and would likely have been very difficult to approach. I finally got him stopped and climbed up into the saddle, my thought was, "Man, the fear this horse has of me is unbelievable."

Now, I knew that I was not the *cause* of that fear. I had no prior relationship with this horse. But I also knew that I was the beneficiary of his fear, and that it was likely a very deep fear.

That fear marked our relationship for the next six months!

It took six months before he would face up to me in his stall, and eventually even walk toward me.

Six months! That is a very long time in the daily training of a horse!

Learning to
"Read" a Horse

Horses are fairly easy to "read." Feeding time is one of the best times to evaluate a horse's attitude. When a horse is hungry, he is usually very glad to see a person show up with a feed bucket. As soon as a person walks into the barn with food, a horse is likely to start nickering—that's a signal that he's glad to see that person.

There are other times, however, when a horse may pin his ears or move to the far side of his stall away from the person with the food bucket. That horse is *not* in a good mood.

At times, the bad mood is not directly related to anything that the person has done. The horse may be upset at something the horse in a neighboring stall has been doing all day, or the fact that the horse in a neighboring stall is being fed *first*.

There are horses that do not want a person to open their stall door. This is often the result of the horse having been mistreated or abused by a person in the past. It can also be the result of the horse experiencing pain to the point that the horse does not want to be touched, and especially not touched in the area of pain. It might be the result of an imbalance of hormones—yes, horses can be and are hormonal!

And in some cases, the horse may just have a bad attitude. That horse may have had that attitude since its birth. It is his *temperament.*

It is up to the human being to figure out *why* a horse is the way he is. And it is especially important to isolate any area of pain, hormonal imbalance, or prior mistreatment. Those are issues that a trainer can and must address. A horse is not going to be able to learn what a trainer is teaching, or acquire discipline in an area, if that horse is struggling with pain or poor health. A horse with prior mistreatment requires *time* and ongoing consistent tenderness, to heal.

Doc Ebonee fit that last category.

Winning the
Battle of Fear

Gypsy made life a pleasant experience for Doc Ebonee. He enjoyed being around her. As a result, he would perform beautifully for her. I wanted that same kind of relationship with Ebonee, and I believed that eventually, as Ebonee began to trust me, he would also begin to enjoy being in my presence.

Gypsy always approached Doc Ebonee slowly, quietly, and with gentleness. She didn't make abrupt movements or reach out to Ebonee with an abrupt gesture.

She dealt with him in a slow and even manner. And Ebonee responded to that. I had to deal with Ebonee in a very quiet way. This was a new challenge for me.

Slow and gentle was not my nature. I certainly wasn't abusive to any horse I've ever trained, but my hand was probably firmer and my hold on the reins stronger, and my legs at the side of the horse more controlling. I came to a new personal realization as I rode Doc Ebonee that my way might not be the *best* way. Up to my work with Ebonee, my way *had* worked. And when it didn't work with Ebonee, I had to back up and rethink and try a new approach.

The same is true in our relationships with people, of course. It takes time, perhaps, for some of us to come to that realization. People may intuitively have a quicker empathy with the "style" of communication, the temperament of personality, or the pace of living that others display. If we want to have a relationship with another person that is longstanding and has depth, we eventually will need to *learn* to accommodate another person's style, temperament, and pace—and in most cases, adjust or adapt our style to be more in sync with theirs.

I'm not saying this is easy. I *am* saying it is reality.

I discovered in the early years of my marriage with Gypsy that the way Gypsy treated the animals she trained was the way she liked to be treated as a human being.

Gypsy didn't approach horses, ponies, her dogs, or other animals in an abrupt, erratic, harsh, impatient, or "forceful" way. And, she did not respond to people who approached her in an abrupt, inconsistent, short-fused, or inconsistent manner. She has no tolerance for people treating her in a rough way—either verbally or physically. If you want to develop a friendship with Gypsy, be gentle, consistent, and kind.

Gypsy is very affectionate toward her horses, and she is affectionate toward the people she calls her friends. If a person has ever hurt Gypsy, however, she is reluctant to give them an opportunity to hurt her again. As a result of her own painful experiences in her young years, she has a great understanding about and empathy with horses who have been mistreated, neglected, or abused.

She has an attitude that the horses pick up on: "I'm *not* going to hurt you. I'm *not* going to be like any person who may have treated you harshly or badly in the past." In her work in the ministry, Gypsy also has that quality. She has a deep heart that reaches out to hurting people, and at the same time, she is quick to try to avoid those who have wounded her or who seem intent on hurting her.

There are many lessons a person can learn about life and relationships by working with horses, but I believe one of the greatest lessons is this: not every horse responds to a trainer in precisely the same way, and conversely, not every method works equally with every horse.

As a pastor, I have come to see this very clearly in the way the Lord leads and guides those who come into relationship with Him. His principles and commands and the precepts of His Word are true, fixed, and absolute. But the application of His Word is individualized for every person. The Lord deals with each of us in a way that works in complete harmony with the personality, dreams, desires, temperament, and purposes He has placed in us. The Lord knows how He has made each one of us, and He always seeks to guide us within the boundaries of His own design. He knows how He made us. He knows how to train us.

> The Lord always seeks to guide us
> within the boundaries of His own
> design. He knows how He made us.
> He knows how to train us.

Our challenge is to treat the people around us as the Lord treats them. We must come to understand how other people have been fashioned by the Lord, and to discern how the Holy Spirit leads them and works in them and through them. We must accommodate others, treating them in the ways that are most beneficial and effective, rather than demanding that others accommodate us at all times and function according to our timetables and methods. We are wise to stand back and see more fully what and how God is working, and then join God in His work rather than demand that others, and God as well, do things "our way."

Much of this insight into horses, people, and life came to me as I worked with Doc Ebonee, and in the years following my work with him.

When I first encountered Doc Ebonee I was not following Jesus as my Savior and Lord. I certainly had no "ministry" or pastoral experiences. For the most part, I was a struggling, hurting person who had fears of my own that were just as deep as those in Doc Ebonee.

3

MY LIFE BEFORE CHRIST

My wife Gypsy was a very good rider, trainer, and exhibitor of cutting horses. Through the months of my knowing her, she had given me an opportunity to ride a couple of her horses and I did nothing but embarrass myself in the cutting-horse pen. I believe the terminology Gypsy used to describe one of my performances was "a wreck." She wasn't being overly critical or mean. She was telling the truth! I couldn't even get my horse to separate a single cow from the herd. In the show-horse world, in the cutting-horse class, that definitely would be the definition of a wreck!

Part of my desire to own Doc Ebonee was to learn *how* to succeed in this area of showing horses that had eluded me. I had experienced success in other categories, and in training the horses of others to succeed in other categories. But not in the cutting-horse class.

There are a couple of things you need to know about me at the time I acquired Doc Ebonee.

First, I was not a believer in Jesus, and therefore, I was not following Him or reading His Word, the Bible. Jesus was not my Savior. He was not my Lord.

Oh, I went to church. I even sang in the choir— mostly because I like to sing and partly because I liked the people in that choir, and also because I liked putting up an image that I was a good person who didn't *need* any more of God than what I already had.

I have discovered through the years that there are a number of pretend-Christians in most churches, and in a significant number of those cases, the man or woman is attending church to avoid being nagged into allowing God into the totality of their life. They are attending in order to keep from being put into a corner of making a decision to *accept* Jesus as Savior or follow Him as Lord. They have just enough church in them to vaccinate them, it seems, from the real deal of knowing the Lord. They are not at all interested in making a firm commitment to *accepting* Jesus. For the most part, they like their lives the way they are and see no need to change. That certainly was my perspective.

Second, I was a man pretty much consumed with the reality of Me, Myself, and I. At the time Doc Ebonee came into my life you could not have fit my ego or arrogance into a football stadium. I was a know-it-all.

I sometimes tell this story to describe myself: A man married a woman who owned a brand-new twenty-volume encyclopedia set. Shortly after their wedding, she put the books up for sale on a radio program. She put a price tag of five dollars on the encyclopedias. When the announcer asked her why she was selling such a fine set of books for such a low price, she replied, "I don't need them now. My husband knows everything." That isn't a *true* story about my marriage with Gypsy, but it could have been!

Do you perceive any need to *change* anything in your life? If not, why not? If so, are you trying to change it all on your own? God wants to help you change.

Control Was a Key Word to Me. Through my growing-up and young adult years, I developed a very deep anger, and felt deep pain about many things. "Control" became a key word in my life. The result was that I sought to control the horses, and sought to control any person I worked alongside in training horses, showing them, and building a business and a reputation as a horse trainer.

My control tendency did not mean, at all, that I did not enjoy horses. The opposite was true.

As a boy, I developed a great love of horses. My brother had a horse, and fortunately for me, I had more time to ride that horse than he had. I longed for the day when I could have a horse of my own. When a horse show came to my town, I was *there!* Even if it meant skipping school.

I liked everything about the horse world. The more I knew about horse shows and the different classes of competition, and saw how horses could be trained to do so many amazing things, the more I wanted to be in that world.

I admired the people who worked in the horse industry. I was impressed by the skill I saw at the horse shows. I wanted to be like those riders and trainers. I wanted the success they enjoyed, or at least displayed to me. There wasn't anything that I wanted other than to be an excellent horseman, and a winning showman.

Everything about the horse world seemed positive and attainable to me.

Being around horses, however, did not keep me from being influenced by my family and neighborhood, which were largely negative and harmful.

The neighborhood in which I grew up had many homes that had lots of pornographic material—not only visual magazines but novels with explicit descriptions. It was a common factor in the lives of the children around me, not just their parents. I was exposed to things at a tender age that I should never have been exposed to.

Once a child is exposed to certain images and information, it is very difficult ever to erase those images from the mind. A chemical reaction in the brain occurs that I don't fully understand, but I know it is real. I know it is addictive.

There was also extensive use of addictive substances in my childhood environment. Smoking and drinking were common—in fact, they were considered signs of male maturity and acceptance. I became addicted to both nicotine and alcohol at an early age, although at the time, nobody talked much about addiction, or even the harmful effects of drinking or using tobacco. These substances were the norm for others around me and they became the norm for me.

I had minimal exposure to church . . . and that was just fine with me.

When I was a boy, one of the things that turned me off about the church was the fact that every time I went to church, it seemed the Sunday school teacher for boys my age would show up at my house during the following weeks, telling me that I needed to attend church and Sunday school *regularly*. It seemed like a heavy-handed approach to me, and I rebelled against that admonition.

Other people in the church seemed insistent on telling me that I needed to accept Jesus as my Savior or that I needed God in my life. I looked at their lives and couldn't help but ask, "Where's the evidence in their lives that shows me it is a good thing to have Jesus as my Savior or to invite God into my life?" There was no discernible difference in the way they lived and the way I was living. There seemed to be no practical benefit, nor did I see any major character differences in their lives.

I frankly saw no reason for accepting Jesus into my life.

And to top it all off, I didn't have much use for school either. In today's world, I would have been classified as ADHD—attention deficit hyperactivity disorder. I did not at all enjoy sitting at a desk in a classroom listening to a teacher drone on about things that were not remotely interesting to me.

I have discovered through the years that I am what is called a "kinetic" learner—I learn by *doing*, far more than by reading, seeing, or even hearing. If someone shows me how to do something, and I can practice it, then I *know* it and never forget it. Other forms of learning aren't nearly as effective with me, and unfortunately, school is long on reading and listening, and short on application and action.

If a boy is subjected to badgering on the one hand about his need to be a better person, and on the other hand, is badgered about his need to be a better student, a very real self-worth issue can develop. By the time I was a young adult, I had very low self-esteem, and I had a general feeling that unless I worked very hard and maintained personal control over as many situations and people as I could, somebody might discover the *real* Tim O'Neal and I'd be doomed. I was fearful of being "found out" as a failure and degenerate person. And those fears, of course, naturally led to bouts with depression.

The addictive substances and activities in my life helped to mask both the fears and depression, but they only created an ongoing cycle of fears and low self-worth producing depression, in turn resulting in self-medication, which in turn led to more fear and a decline in self-value.

CONTROL was vital! I felt an ongoing *demand* to be in control.

A Success
Nonetheless

It is rather amazing to me in retrospect to realize that neither my aversion to school or to church seemed to matter when it came to rising through the ranks in the horse industry. With horses, I could learn and *do*—all of the necessary skills were rooted in behavior and application. Many of the people in the horse world drank and used tobacco as much as I did. I developed a skill in using foul language and telling dirty stories—in fact, I have joked through the years that I earned a Ph.D. in those fields. Rather than tarnish my reputation, my witty sarcasm, cynicism, foul language, and dirty stories seemed to make me acceptable to many people and respected trainers whom I met in the horse industry.

My "outside" person was a person who was generally considered *successful.* And, I was winning more and more awards, and money, at the shows.

At the time I met Gypsy, I was a horse trainer living in Madisonville, Texas. I had never married and I had grown accustomed to a single life—I had only Me, Myself, and I to deal with, and for the most part, that suited me.

I am quite sure that I had not considered that "stress" might be a potential   factor in a marriage relationship. I just knew that I admired Gypsy—and yes, loved her—and I wanted to marry her. Gypsy had two teenage children when we married; they were in high school. I got along with them fine and didn't see any problem at all in adopting them and taking on the role of "dad."

If I could project an image of success in my career, surely I could project that same image as a family man.

Almost immediately after we married, Gypsy became pregnant, which meant a baby in the house—something I discovered was different than having two teenagers in the house.

I truly loved each person who had come into my life in a very short space of time. But I was also aware that I was experiencing increased stress. There was more and more to "control" and I didn't feel as if I was doing a very good job of control. Feeling overwhelmed was a new emotion for me, and with that feeling came *added* stress and discouragement. The discouragement spiraled down into depression. The more I tried to be "in control," the less I was.

I'm not at all blaming Gypsy, the children, or the institution of marriage. I'm just admitting that so many changes in such a short amount of time knocked my equilibrium for a loop.

To compound matters, I seemed to have fewer people wanting my services as a trainer—there were no specific reasons, just one of those ebb and flow times in a career when old clients move on, and new clients have not yet arrived. Even so, my self-esteem was impacted, although I certainly would not have admitted that to Gypsy or to anyone else. I became seriously depressed.

I was hurting deeply, but I could not have told you or anyone precisely *why* I was hurting, or precisely what had caused my pain. I have learned through the years that most people who are depressed don't really *know* why they are feeling so down—they are just down. Emotional pain is not hard to recognize, but it is very difficult to *diagnose*—to pinpoint why a person is feeling hurt, and then to know how to heal the hurt.

Very often, the emotional pain or depression has been brewing or festering in the person for a long time, perhaps just under the surface of everyday emotions and reactions. Something in early childhood may have set the pain or depression in motion, and through the years, additional events, encounters, or circumstantial problems may have added to the pain or discouragement. In nearly all cases, there are multiple inner wounds in a person's life, each adding a bit to the pain until it is, as one counselor once told me, like a coffee mug being filled one drop at a time until one day, the mug is full and just one more drop sends the contents of the mug over the edge of the mug.

I knew *some* of the issues and difficulties I had experienced in my growing-up years, but I couldn't even remember *all* of the issues and difficulties. I just knew that I had reached a point of misery and deep discouragement . . . and I needed to find a way out of my pain.

Taking the Move
to Get Help

One time when I was competing in a cutting event, my horse went to the left and he suddenly stopped, threw his head up, and *quit!* I was furious. One of the handlers said, "You need to take him out back and beat him for quitting on you that way."

Gypsy stepped in and said, "No, we're going to take him to the vet. That horse is no quitter. There's something seriously wrong with him. That horse is hurting somewhere and we need to find a horse chiropractor and see what's wrong."

In the middle of that stop and turn, the horse had whinnied just a little. I'm not sure anybody else heard him, but I did. Even so, I was upset at losing the entry fee—we

31

were living pretty much hand to mouth at that time and I had expected to win some money with that horse—but I also knew from that slight nicker that something could be wrong. The horse had never stopped like that before, and he didn't have an overall temperament to do something like that.

It just so happened that the most famous horse chiropractor of that time was in the town where that cutting event was being held. We called him and he said he had time to see the horse, so we took the horse over to him that evening and he worked on him and adjusted him. The next day, that horse worked beautifully and gave his best effort and performance.

If we had not listened to that horse, or if we had taken the advice of other people around us, the problem would *not* have been resolved, and certainly not through any heavy-handed means. We had to read the signs we could read and act on them, on behalf of the horse. The horse could not tell us his specific problem. It was up to us to determine that the problem was physical—not an act of rebellion.

That was pretty much the same state in which I found myself—I was hurting deeply. It stopped me in my tracks. And I needed help.

I resisted reaching out for help, of course . . . until the depression and inner pain became too great.

I finally made the decision to check myself into Rapha, a psychiatric facility in Bryan, Texas.

> Emotional pain is not hard
> to recognize, but it is very
> difficult to *diagnose.*

4

A NEW WAY OF LIFE

I had been accepted at Rapha as a person who needed help battling clinical depression. Depression was actually something that I had a long history of experiencing. I had experienced rejection from a friend in my early teen years. That feeling of rejection and abandonment was compounded by my low self-esteem and attention-deficit problems—which resulted in poor school performance, which only served to compound my esteem issues. Add to that my stubborn attempts at self-justification and blame, and also my deep feelings of guilt and shame. It was no mystery at all that I was *depressed*.

The trouble is, if you are the one who is depressed, you are generally too close to a tree to see the bigger forest.

I needed help in discovering *why* I was depressed, and then, what to do about it.

I was very grateful for my counselors Steve and Sam who helped me sort out so many things from my past. They helped me to see that yes, I had been *abused*. Any person who leaves pornography lying around where a child can see it is being abusive to that child. Anyone who inappropriately fondles a child is abusing that child sexually, mentally, and emotionally. My counselors helped me also to see that I had continued to abuse *myself*. There comes a point where a person must be willing to make the tough choices to *change* the pattern of what has been done to him in the past. They helped me see that I was responsible for my life *now*, and moving forward. I needed to make decisions, and do so with a firm commitment, to define and then pursue the life I truly wanted.

I don't recommend counseling lightly. But I do recommend *godly, Christ-centered* counseling as a wonderful opportunity for a person who is willing to take responsibility for his life and make the tough choices to change, grow, and pursue renewal.

In addition to tackling my depression, my counselors gave me valuable insight into the nature of stress, and how to cope with the stress I had been feeling. I learned there are many causes for stress, many manifestations of it, and a number of cures related to it. Sometimes other people put pressure on us to do more than we can do—either we don't yet have the skills necessary, or we may not have the mental or physical energy for the level of performance others may want from us. Sometimes deadlines are too quick for us to do our best. The important thing was to discover what I, Tim, had internalized as stress.

The truth is, we need to become our own best expert on what causes us to feel stress and ask God to show us ways to avoid stress or deal with it. I am firmly convinced that God *wants* us to live in peace—the Word of God tells us this repeatedly. He wants us to live without fear and anxiety—again, God's Word tells us this again and again. If you struggle with this, ask God to give you His confidence and His insight into how to deal with stress.

> We each must become our own best
> expert on what causes us to feel
> stress—and then ask God to show us
> ways to avoid stress or deal with it.

Along the way, of course, I was being helped to detox my body from all the chemicals I had been pouring into it. Smoking, drinking, dipping snuff, and taking addictive heavy-duty prescription drugs were *not* allowed at Rapha. That was difficult at a physical level, but it was no more difficult than confronting my inner struggles and emotions. Rapha was the most intense uphill learning curve I had ever faced in my life—all of it for my good, but all of it very difficult.

The Spiritual Dimension
to Getting Well

Rapha is a Christ-centered psychiatric program, and as you might readily conclude, there was a great deal of spiritual counseling to accompany the psychological therapy I received. My counselors were unashamedly bold in presenting Jesus to me as Savior and Lord. While I may not have been open to all that had been said to me about Jesus in the past, I was grateful *now* for what they said. Through the years a number of people had been very willing to drag me to any number of religious meetings to accept Jesus, or to push me toward a church altar for that purpose. But it wasn't until it became MY desire to know Him that I could make that decision and mean the commitment I was making.

My counselors knew that. They gave me all the room I needed to make my own decision.

Steve was the foremost counselor assigned to me at the rehab center as my *personal* counselor. We had a number of conversations during the first week and a half. At the center of every conversation was Jesus, and about a person's need to accept the help that only Jesus could offer. He laid out very clearly what it meant to accept Jesus as *Savior*, and how to do it. He alluded to a life led by the Holy Spirit that involved following Jesus as *Lord*. Much of what he said went in one ear and out the next. But little kernels of what he said landed on my hurting heart.

I did know *some things* about Jesus.

My brother had talked to me about Jesus and my need to be saved. I was twenty-four years old at the time. I remember the conversation vividly, and at the end of it, I prayed with my brother to receive Jesus as my Savior. The difference between that prayer and my life as I entered Rapha is that I was now *ready* to hear about Jesus.

Every person grows at their own pace. Every person comes to decisions in their own way. Our role must be to encourage others and to be a role model for them of a life in Christ Jesus. We must never throw another person under the bus and declare them "hopeless" or "worthless." We must never hound a person in a way that becomes obnoxious. We must always keep the doors of the church open, and the doors of our heart open, to be used by God in the ways the LORD defines and directs.

I received a great deal of wisdom at Rapha, but there really was no hard-pressure sell to receive Jesus. My counselors wanted me to know that they believed He was vital to life, and they wanted me to know *how* to receive Jesus and to know *what* the consequences of that decision would be . . . but there was no pressure or hard sell.

An Insistence about Responsibility. What my counselors did *insist* that I do was accept responsibility for my life. I was challenged to face up to my own role for creating the mess I was in. I had never done that before. I had always justified that I was right, others were wrong. Or I had blamed others for my problems, refusing to admit my role in harboring those problems once I was an adult. I faced up to all this with the help of my counselors there. I didn't *like* being responsible for the mess of my life, but I knew I had to own up to the fact that it was *my life* and my doing.

Another way of saying this, more in keeping with the church view of things, is that I had to face up to the fact that my sinful life was *mine*. I had to confess that I was a sinner in need of a savior. I had to own up to the fact that I had made serious mistakes and had rebelled against God, and I needed to make new decisions if I was going to experience a new life.

They say a mark of insanity is doing the same things over and over and expecting new results. The reality is, doing the same things over and over is going to take us to the same results—every time. I needed to stop doing what I had been doing—and thinking and saying—if I was going to experience a new sense of peace and fulfillment.

Dealing with Guilt. My counselors also insisted that I come to grip with the guilt I felt over things I had done wrong in the past. I was haunted by some of my old behaviors and felt in bondage to the memory of some of my old relationships. No matter how much I told myself that I shouldn't feel guilty, or didn't want to feel guilty, *I felt guilty!* I had a deep longing to get rid of the guilt, and yes, shame.

Let me assure you of this, believing in Jesus began to seem more and more like the solution to both issues— owning up to my personal responsibility, and being set free from guilt and shame.

> Are you taking responsibility for your life, and ALL your actions? Have you discovered the way to be free of all guilt and shame?

Thinking about a Horse
Named Doc Ebonee . . .

Shortly before I entered Rapha, I had competed in the American Quarter Horse World Championship show. I had shown Ebonee in the senior cutting. We had ordered a videotape of my runs with Doc Ebonee, and Gypsy brought a copy of that video to the clinic so I could see it.

I had placed fifth in that competition. That was a respectable showing, but it wasn't the best I could do or Doc Ebonee could do. Rather than see our runs in a positive light, I saw them in a more negative light. Even so, just seeing Doc Ebonee on the television monitor reminded me of all that I had been through with Ebonee, and how the horse had come to trust me and help me BECOME a better rider.

That night I began to reflect back over my life and what I had learned at the rehab center thus far. I reflected on what it had taken for Doc Ebonee to learn to trust me. And I came to a conclusion: If Doc Ebonee could learn to trust me, then surely I could learn to trust what most people seemed to believe is the most powerful Thing in the universe—JESUS.

I went to the nurses' station later that evening and asked them to call my counselor. It was late, long after normal hospital hours, but the Rapha clinic had a policy that *any time* a patient wanted to have a visit from a counselor, a counselor would come. The counselor came. I called him by name and said, "You have been talking to me about Jesus for the last week and a half. I don't understand all that you've told me, but if asking Jesus into my life will change my life and bring peace into my life, I'm ready to do that . . . right now."

He was surprised, delighted, and we began to pray together immediately. This time I truly *meant* what I was praying.

I knew that to accept Jesus as my Savior meant confessing that I was a sinner in need of a Savior. I did that.

I knew that my acceptance of Jesus meant a total commitment and surrender of my life to Him. I made that commitment.

I knew I was not only accepting Jesus as my Savior, but also accepting that Jesus was my LORD. He was going to be the One I served, the One who "owned" me because He had redeemed me, the One who was worthy of my devotion and praise, the One who was sending the Holy Spirit into my life to lead and guide me. I made a declaration that I was ready for that.

Repentance means a "turn-around." It means a change. And there are people who say they repent and receive Jesus, but in truth, we do the CHANGING after we have received God's forgiveness and the Holy Spirit who will help us to change! We confess that we need a Savior and that we believe Jesus is God's appointed Savior, and we ask Jesus to be our Savior and to cleanse us from our sin and bring us into full reconciliation with God the Father. That's our part.

God's part is to cleanse us from sin, give us the Holy Spirit, and help us to CHANGE—to renew our minds by reading the Word of God, to change our behavior by applying the Word of God, and to pursue a new lifestyle according to the principles of the Word of God. Repentance is ongoing. God's forgiveness is ongoing. And our awareness that we are following Jesus as our LORD must also be ongoing. I knew I was embarking on a process of change. I wanted change.

I say that I *knew* all of these things on the night that I prayed with a Rapha counselor named Steve. In truth, I only saw broad outlines of those truths. I didn't know all that was involved . . . but I did know this with certainty: I didn't want to continue to live the way I had been living. I wanted a new life!

A Total Transformation
in Body and Spirit!

That night, in the wake of my prayer to receive Jesus as my Savior and Lord, I experienced a genuine transformation in my life—both physically and spiritually.

My desires shifted one hundred and eighty degrees. My old life was not my *new* life.

I went into Rapha smoking four packs of cigarettes a day, and dipping two cans of Skoal a day. I had been drinking as much as I could in a day, and drinking large amounts of alcohol-based sleeping medications at night. I went into Rapha with depression, a ton of anxiety, and a pattern of self-loathing. I cussed a blue streak and had a great repertoire of filthy jokes and stories. All of that PLUS depression and emotional anxiety and suicidal thoughts. I was a mess.

I prayed with that counselor and gave my life to Jesus, accepting Him as my Savior and Lord, and the moment I said "Amen" to that prayer . . . I immediately lost all desire for tobacco in all forms, all desire for alcohol in any form, and all desire for the prescription drugs I had been taking. I no longer wanted to tell filthy jokes and stories, and I stopped swearing.

I was finally able to take responsibility for my sinful self, confess my sin to Christ, and know with certainty that He had washed away my sin in a way that brought total cleansing. God's Word says that if we confess our sin, He is faithful to forgive us our sin, and to cleanse us from all unrighteousness [sinfulness]. (See 1 John 1:9.) That's God's promise and I accepted it as His promise to me!

I was also set free spiritually from bondage to guilt and shame.

I know what it is like to feel dirty, and I now know what it is like to feel clean. Clean is so much better! Many people accommodate a certain amount of "dirt" in their lives. I don't want any of it. I want purity and nothing but purity.

More importantly, I had a peace in my heart, and a hope for my future. I didn't know all that it meant to call Jesus my Savior, and I had even less idea what it meant to call Jesus the Lord of my life, but I was willing to embark on the journey to find out. I had no doubt that Jesus had entered my life in a profound way. I had meant my prayer of accepting Him—all the way to the core of my soul—and I believed without any hesitation or second-guessing that Jesus had become my Savior and Lord.

I am aware that many people are not delivered immediately from their addictions in the way I was. I am grateful for my experience and I know it is a miracle from God—it was an act of God's *deliverance*, not just a healing of my mind or body.

New Challenges for
a Changed Man

I was changed from the inside out, but I still faced the challenge of changing the habits and routines of my life, including the habits of my *thought life*. I knew spiritually that I was delivered, but my mind wanted to take me back to my past. I realized that I had to guard myself continually against temptations to fall back into some of those old addictive behaviors.

One of the things I had struggled with throughout my young life—beginning as a boy and on through my teenage years—was a habit of looking at pornography. I was delivered from all desire to pursue that habit when I accepted Jesus. But I also assure you that I know I must never "test" my deliverance in that area. I need to exert my will to stay as far away from anything lewd or pornographic as possible.

The same holds true when it comes to alcohol, tobacco, and addictive prescription drugs. My desires had to change—not just my habits.

I have come to the point today, decades later, where I have no desire to go where alcohol, tobacco, or addictive substances are sold or used extensively. I have no desire to go into bars. I have no desire to watch movies or television programs that depict the use of substances that I know from personal experience have been harmful to me in my past. And, I have no desire to keep alcohol, tobacco, or addictive medications in a back cupboard somewhere "just in case."

My deliverance was instantaneous. My ongoing abstinence is a combination of my faith and my will. I *want* to follow Jesus. I *want* the life He gives. I *want* to be the man God created me to be and fulfill the purpose He has for my life. And I do NOT want any distractions or addictive substances of any kind that might trip me up on my walk with the Lord.

There are many people who think I go overboard in abstaining from even *looking* at programs in which there is sexual innuendo, instances of adultery or illicit sexual behavior, or use of drugs and alcohol. Not to mention the sarcasm and criticism and behaviors that cover a spectrum of "cheating" attitudes and sneaky dealings. The fact is, these things are supernaturally repulsive to me.

My wife Gypsy has said on occasion, "Tim won't even watch 'I Love Lucy'!" She's right! Stop to consider the plot and dialog of many of the Lucy episodes. Many of them are about "cheating" or lying or engaging in fraudulent dealings in some form. One of the most famous episodes is about getting drunk. All for the purpose of getting a laugh. Well, for me, that lifestyle was nothing to laugh about. It was something to get serious about. I was on a path to an early grave and I have a deep appreciation that I was set free to walk a path that promises abundant life and eternal life. I have no desire to turn around!

My request to my family members and friends has been, "I'm asking you to *help* me walk the life I know is right for me. I've been there and done that when it comes to what I now know was harmful to my soul. Help me walk in a way that I know is right for my soul."

Thinking New Thoughts. I am fully aware that a person cannot think about two things at the same time. A person cannot think about negative, lustful, illicit images and behaviors, and think about the Word of God simultaneously. The more I began to fill my mind with a knowledge of God's Word, and began to memorize and speak God's Word often—and then more often, and then more often—the more my brain began to be rewired to think godly thoughts and to hate ungodly ones.

A person who has read a fair bit about the addictive processes of the brain confirmed to me during a conversation about this that the brain creates an "alternative route" the more it is steeped in God's truth. The old route of thinking, that was once automatic and almost instinctual, is still there, but it is like an abandoned highway that isn't used by the believer who truly wants to develop a new route to a new destination.

Let me encourage you—it *is* possible *not* to think the way you used to think, or may presently be thinking. It *is* possible for you to develop a new pathway in your own brain that exalts God and takes you to a destination that God honors. The Bible refers to this as the *renewal* (changing) of a person's mind. (See Romans 12:2–3.) God the Holy Spirit desires to do that renewing work in the life of every person.

My wife Gypsy was not addicted to the things that had me in their grip. I am very thankful for that. But Gypsy had her own issues to deal with. She had been badly abused by a man from her early teen years until her late twenties. She had been filled with guilt and fear. Her abuser had died before I met Gypsy, but she, too, was in a process of "getting free" during those early months and years of our marriage.

She was rewiring her brain, too, to accommodate the TRUTH of God's Word and to choose to live according to it. She had old thinking that needed to be turned into new thinking by the Holy Spirit. She, too, was undergoing a renewal process.

In many ways, this was beneficial to us as a couple. We both understood that we had been caught up in the grip of things that were not godly, and were not God's desire for us as individuals. We both understood that only the Holy Spirit could truly set us free and give us the spiritual power to resist old temptations and walk out a new life. We both knew that it was vitally important that we immerse ourselves in the Word of God in order to live the new life we wanted.

Criticism and sarcasm did not fall away as quickly as the more physical habits. My moving beyond criticism and sarcasm has been a lifelong journey. So much of our media programming is steeped with critical and sarcastic commentary, with characters putting one another down in order to evoke laughter. It seems to me at times that our entire culture has low self-esteem to the point that we are all trying to build ourselves up by tearing one another down. I knew a lot about that tactic, of course. By the time I went to Rapha, I had an advanced degree in low self-esteem and a great deal of skill in "cutting" people down to size with my sarcasm and witty cynicism.

From the time I left Rapha, I had a strong desire to know more about the commitment I had made to follow Jesus as my Savior and Lord.

What did it really MEAN to call Jesus as my Savior?

What did it really MEAN to follow Jesus as my Lord?

And HOW did Jesus as Savior and Lord impact my thinking and my speaking?

I was eager to discover answers!

5

TRUSTING IN JESUS AS SAVIOR

A person who heard me tell my story about Doc Ebonee and my experience at Rapha once asked me, "Are you telling me that a horse led you to the Lord?" Another person once asked, "Are you saying that Doc Ebonee 'saved' you?"

The answer is NO to both questions. A counselor at Rapha told me about Jesus and prayed with me to receive Jesus into my life. The Holy Spirit is the One who convicted me of my sin and my need for a Savior.

But . . . a horse *was* used by God to show me the importance of trust and to give me the confidence that I *could* trust Jesus with my life and my future.

That has been a pattern I've experienced often during the three decades since I accepted Jesus. God has used a horse to teach me a principle, and then He has shown me how that principle has a *spiritual meaning*. My work with horses has been a bridge-making process between the natural world and the spiritual world, revealing truths to me and making them crystal clear. What I've learned from the horses runs parallel with what I read and understand about the Word of God.

Some people have seemed to be offended when I have said that Doc Ebonee was a key element in my coming to know the Lord as my Savior. They have thought I was giving credit to the horse for my spiritual transformation. Not at all! Doc Ebonee was *used* to reveal to me the truth that I *could* learn to submit my life to Jesus and trust Him moving forward after I left the rehab center.

If you have never received Jesus as your Savior, you may have some questions about the use of this word *savior*—or about "salvation" or what it means to be "saved." Let me take a few paragraphs to give you some basics.

The Bible teaches that salvation comes from trusting Jesus as the Christ, or the Savior. Romans 10:9 says that if a person confesses with their mouth that Jesus is Lord, and believes in their heart that God raised Him from the dead, that person is "saved"—or given complete forgiveness of their sins and granted eternal life.

The next verse (10:10) sums it up saying it is by believing with your heart that you are made right with God, and by confession with your mouth that we are saved. Romans 10:13 assures us that any person who calls upon the name of the Lord shall be saved.

I want you to note that phrase, "believing with the heart." In our world today, the heart is often confused with emotions, or affection, or love. While we certainly should come to love God, believing with the heart in Bible times was not something rooted in a person's emotions. The heart was considered the seat of the *will*. Doing something with the heart meant to do it with intention, a focus of the will, and with a deep, firm commitment. We come into relationship with Jesus as our Savior as an act of our *will*, and with a commitment that is resolute and lasting.

I had a huge need to be "saved" in my life. I needed to be rescued from my own bad choices and decisions. I needed to be rescued from deep depression, anxiety, and low self-worth. I needed to be rescued from an ocean of guilt and shame. I needed to be snatched out of the devil's clutches and delivered from a bondage to sin—the feeling that I was trapped by sin and that I lived with an inevitability about sin. I *knew* I was in bondage to things that

Tim, Mr. Control, could *not* control. I could not deliver myself. I had tried, continually and repeatedly, and nothing was as absolute or as transformative as the power of God entering into me on the night I received Jesus as my Savior.

I had tried to manage my own life for many years, and had come to realize that I could not succeed in this management job on my own! I needed help from outside myself. I needed someone to rescue me and help me. In all ways that mattered most, I needed "saving" from myself!

Human Effort Is Never Enough. Salvation is not something any person can earn or achieve or accomplish. Salvation is a gift *from God.* It is a free gift given to every person who is willing to receive it. It is a gift that includes a cleansing by God from sin, guilt, and shame. It is a gift that ensures us that we are fully reconciled to God as a beloved son or daughter. It is also a gift that ensures us that we are the recipients of eternal life.

After God gave the Ten Commandments to the Jews, along with other laws that we can read about in the first five books of the Old Testament, the Jewish leaders began to add their interpretation of the Law of Moses. Through the centuries before Jesus' life on this earth, the religious leaders added more than four hundred laws that they said were essential for a person to be in right standing with God.

They believed that human effort, no matter how sincere, could bring a person into a position of acceptance by God.

Through the centuries, however, more and more people came to know from personal trial and failure that *no* human effort could cleanse the human heart. No matter how grand or "perfect" a personal discipline for good may seem in human eyes, it is not sufficient. No person is capable of saying "no" to all sin, every minute of an entire lifetime. God's Word makes it very clear that ALL people have sinned and that we are kidding ourselves if we think otherwise.

There are two verses that underscore this truth:

- "For all have sinned and fall short of the glory of God." (Romans 3:23) This passage goes on to say that we are justified, or put in right standing with God "as a gift of His grace through the redemption which is in Christ Jesus." (Romans 3:24 NAS)

- "If we say that we have no sin, we are deceiving ourselves and the truth is not in us." (1 John 1:8 NAS)

Jesus made it very clear that no matter how much a person may have kept the commands of the Law, the only way to be in full right standing and reconciliation with God was through accepting Jesus as the Son of God *by faith.*

Faith is another word for believing. Every person has the ability to believe. The Bible teaches us that a "measure" of faith has been given to every person—and even if we have a very small measure of ability to believe, it is sufficient for believing that Jesus is the Son of God. It is that believing that leads to our salvation.

Jesus Is the Only Qualified Savior. Jesus said, "For God so loved the world that He gave His only begotten Son, that whoever *believes* in Him, should not perish but have everlasting life." (John 3:16, italics added for emphasis) Every person *can* fall into the "whoever" category if he or she chooses! God's Word also says, "For the wages of sin is death, but the free gift of God is *eternal life* in Christ Jesus our Lord." (Romans 6:23 NAS, italics added for emphasis)

The Bible tells us very clearly that Jesus was the only One—the only begotten Son of God—who could pay the sacrifice required to take us from the clutches of sin and place us squarely in the hands of God for forgiveness, mercy, and full reconciliation.

Jesus is the *only* person who lived a truly sinless life. Even those who persecuted Jesus admitted that no sin could be found in Him, and that He was a man without any guile, which is cunning deceit. The death of Jesus—God the Son—on the cross was God's means of offering *Himself* as the sacrifice that can take a person from being a *sinful* person to a *saved* person. Jesus made it very clear in saying, "I am the way, and the truth, and the life; no one comes to the Father but through Me." (John 14:6 NAS)

The Bible gives this incredibly wonderful promise to us: "If we confess our sins, He is faithful and righteous to forgive us our sins and to cleanse us from all unrighteousness." (1 John 1:9 NAS)

We can be forgiven!

We can be cleansed!

We can receive the gift of eternal life!

We can experience genuine transformation in our spirit!

Our part is to confess to God that we are sinners in need of a Savior, and to accept or believe that Jesus is the Savior sent to us by God. We are to accept the salvation that Jesus offers to us as God's free gift, and to commit ourselves to believing in Jesus with our whole heart.

God's part is to be true to His own plan and purpose—His own Word—and to save us from the devil, save us from ourselves, and save us from the bondage of sin.

Now I certainly did not know all that I have said on these last few pages the night that I accepted Jesus as my Savior. I prayed with the counselor at Rapha as an act of my will, choosing to *believe* or to have *faith* that Jesus would be my Savior. I made a commitment of accepting Him into my life, and a commitment to following Him according to His Word, the Bible, no matter what.

I was eager to discover what it meant to follow Jesus as LORD.

6

FOLLOWING JESUS AS LORD

On the night that I prayed with faith to receive Jesus as my Savior, I had a very deep and abiding *knowing* that He would be my absolute, irreplaceable, always-present Savior from that day forward. He couldn't be *more* of a Savior to me than He was in that moment, or in this present moment. Jesus made it very clear to His followers that He would *never* leave them nor forsake them. Rather, He promised that He would be with them always, even to the end of time. He said to His followers: "Lo, I am with you, even to the end of the age." (Matthew 28:20 NAS)

Jesus also promised that He would send the Holy Spirit to those who accepted Him as God's Son and received Him as their Savior. Here are some of the things Jesus said about the Holy Spirit, whom He also called the "Helper" and the "Spirit of Truth":

- "I will ask the Father, and He will give you another Helper, that He may be with you forever; that is the Spirit of truth. . . . I will not leave you as orphans; I will come to you." (John 14:16–18 NAS)

- "When the Helper comes, whom I will send to you from the Father, that is the Spirit of truth who proceeds from the Father, He will testify about Me." (John 15:26 NAS)

- "When He, the Spirit of truth, comes, He will guide you into all the truth; for He will not speak on His own initiative, but whatever He hears, He will speak; and He will disclose to you what is to come. He will glorify Me, for He will take of Mine, and will disclose it to you." (John 16:13–14 NAS)

Jesus taught that the Holy Spirit has a number of specific roles. He is our Comforter, who assures us that we are forgiven and in relationship with God the Father. He is our Counselor, reminding us of the words of Jesus and leading us into the right paths in which we are to walk out our lives. He is our "dunamis," a Greek word for power; the Holy Spirit empowers us to live a godly life and to reject sinful temptations.

The Holy Spirit enables us to follow Jesus as our Lord.

What Does It Mean to
Have a "Lord"?

What does it mean to have a lord for your life? Most people in our world today do not have the same understanding for the word *lord* as people in Bible times. Slavery was very common in the first century. Many people had slaves, some of who were almost like family members. Other people had indentured servants, who were working off a debt or obligation. A "lord" was a person who had authority over slaves or servants.

If you were a servant or slave, you looked to your "lord" to map out your day—telling you the work you were to do, where you were to go, and how you were to do your work and live your life as a servant under his authority. The "lord" was responsible for protecting you as long as you kept the laws of the land and the rules of his household or estate. The "lord" provided for you the food, shelter, and clothing you needed. The "lord" established the rules for relationships you might have with other servants or slaves, and also relationships with a person who might become your spouse or the children you might bear while living under his authority. A slave or servant had very little decision-making responsibility—in fact, the only real decision a slave could make was to say "yes" or "no" to what his lord commanded or allowed.

A good servant or slave was usually treated well by Jewish owners. A good lord followed the commandments of the Law, which stated that the slaves or servants in the lord's household were to be given the same privileges related to the Sabbath, Jewish feasts, and religious rituals. Jewish slave owners were expected to treat their servants with respect, and Jewish slaves were commanded by God's Word to treat their owners with respect and to work diligently and consistently as a sign of respect. Slaves or servants under Roman rule were seldom treated as well, or with as much respect.

In the New Testament, the apostle Paul and others stated that *they* were "bondservants" to Christ. They were under His lordship. Everything that applied to good owner-slave relationships in the natural, material world of that time, also applied spiritually to those who were following Jesus. He was to be their LORD.

Jesus also called Himself "Lord" as He taught His disciples during the last supper He shared with them before His crucifixion. He said: "You call Me Teacher and Lord; and you are right, for so I am." (John 13:13 NAS)

As their LORD, Jesus had authority for telling His followers where to go, what to do, how to live, and when to act. He provided for and protected His followers. He expected their loyalty and their diligence in doing the work

He authorized them to do. He established the principles for their good relationships with God the Father and all other Christians. Jesus was in authority over those who were His disciples, and their respect for Him was to be manifested with praise, worship, and obedience to His commands.

Receiving Directives
from Jesus Our Lord

How does Jesus communicate with us as the Lord of our lives? He does it in two ways.

First, we have the Bible. The written Word of God, which includes the example of JESUS as the "Word of God," is one of two main ways Jesus communicates with us today.

The commands of Jesus do not negate or overturn the commands of the Old Testament that are related to right and wrong, or the way we are to live out our daily lives. Rather than replace the Old Testament commands, Jesus expanded upon them—He made them a matter of the heart, not just outer behavior. Jesus fulfilled all of the Old Testament laws related to blood sacrifice, but He said about the laws that deal with worship and human relationships that He did not come to change the commandments, but to *fulfill* them. In Jesus we see the perfect example of *how* to live in right relationship with God the Father.

Jesus commanded that we love God with our whole heart, soul, and mind. (See Matthew 22:37.) He commanded that we love our neighbors as we love ourselves. (Matthew 22:39) Even if we don't understand anything other than those two statements—which are actually quotations by Jesus of the Old Testament—that's enough to keep us busy for a lifetime!

We also read in the Bible the commands of Jesus to love one another as our brothers and sisters in Christ. He said, "A new commandment I give to you, that you love one another, even as I have loved you, that you also love one another. By this all men will know that you are My disciples, if you have love for one another." (John 13:34–35 NAS)

Jesus made it very clear, "If you love Me, you will keep My commandments." (John 14:15 NAS) He also said, "He who has My commandments and keeps them is the one who loves Me; and he who loves Me will be loved by My Father, and I will love him and will disclose Myself to him." (John 14:21 NAS)

Second, we have the Holy Spirit resident in us to communicate the desires of God the Father and Jesus the Son to us.

Romans 12:2 (NAS) tells us that we are not to be "conformed to this world, but be transformed by the renewing of your mind, so that you may prove what the will of God is, that which is good and acceptable and perfect." It is the Holy Spirit resident in us who teaches us precisely what is

- GOOD—the right way to live. The Holy Spirit clearly teaches us and gives us evidence for what is right, versus what is wrong, in God's eyes.
- ACCEPTABLE—the paths of life that God honors. The Holy Spirit guides us into the paths that produce righteousness, blessing, and favor with God.
- PERFECT—what is exactly right for each one of us. The Holy Spirit directs us in ways we are to use our God-given talents and spiritual gifts. He leads us into avenues of service and worship to the Lord that produce the maximum amount of fulfillment, satisfaction, and joy.

The Holy Spirit was not sent to us to limit us, but rather, to help us focus our lives for maximum effectiveness and productivity. The Holy Spirit shows us the way to live so we can sidestep the devil's traps and temptations. He gives us godly goals. He empowers us with creative ideas and the best methods for accomplishing the tasks God gives us. In all ways, the Holy Spirit helps us follow in the footsteps of Jesus. He turns us into disciples of Jesus who are obeying Jesus fully as the Lord of our lives!

The Irreplaceable Value
of the Word of God

It is very important that we read and study the Bible so that we can learn who God is, what Jesus has done for us, and who we have become and are now in the process of becoming in Christ Jesus. The Bible is our foremost teacher. The Holy Spirit confirms the truth of God's Word, shows us how to apply God's Word, and gives us the ability to apply God's Word. The Holy Spirit brings the Bible alive!

My spiritual journey in Jesus as LORD truly took off when I realized that I could LEARN the Word of God and that this would be the foundation for trusting God every day and walking in the ways that were pleasing to God.

Up to that point in my life, I had trusted the world systems about who I was to be as a man. I had trusted in my own thinking and reasoning ability. After I accepted Jesus as my Savior, and had set out to follow Jesus as my Lord, I discovered that much of what I had trusted was deficient, limited, or outright false. I had to *relearn* most of life so that it might be grounded on the truth of God's Word. I felt many times as if I was just a baby, learning how to walk and talk and respond to life in the right ways.

As humbling as it was to discover all the ways I had been *wrong*, it was also exciting to discover all the new ways that were *right,* and to know with certainty that God was not only with me, but that His Holy Spirit was in me to help me make the *right* choices in the right timing, all for the right reasons and results!

As I reflected on my relationship with Ebonee during the months I was riding him, I recognized that my time with that horse had been marked by two major concepts: steady gentle training, and fellowship.

Steady Gentle Training. Doc Ebonee and I worked together every day, for different lengths of time at different tasks. I was patient, even-handed, and steady. I had to *learn* patience and kindness, which combined to create "steady."

I admit that it wasn't always *easy* to be gentle and patient, but I had been in the horse-showing world long enough to know that if I was harsh or impatient, we would be taking two or three steps backward and it would be an even longer process for Doc Ebonee to trust me.

Doc Ebonee had to teach me the "Ebonee" way of doing things. I needed to learn more about his instincts and innate abilities.

Fellowship. There were times when Doc Ebonee and I did not work directly on a specific command or task. People might characterize those times as "just hanging out." In times of fellowship I was not following a training agenda. Rather, I was simply spending time with him, getting him accustomed to me even as I became accustomed to him. We often rode for the "fun" of it.

It was a combination of steady gentle training and "fellowship" that led Doc Ebonee to trust me.

The more Ebonee trusted me, the more he relaxed around me. He began to come to me rather than run from me.

In many ways, that is what STARTED to happen within me at Rapha. During the days I was there, I saw how God worked through the Christian counselors on the Rapha staff. They were steady, kind, and patient with me. They encouraged me. They didn't belittle me, criticize me, or make me feel foolish for things I had done or thought in my past. They seemed to enjoy being around me and made me feel valuable and loved. I was a person to them, not a "patient."

Most of all, they presented Jesus to me as a source of love—of healing, strength, and blessing. They modeled before me how good it was to have Jesus as Savior and Lord. In them I could see the confidence, humility, and genuine benefit that came from being in a personal relationship with God the Father through Jesus, His Son.

I wanted to follow in their footsteps because I could see they were following in the footsteps of Jesus. He was their LORD. And I was willing for Him to become my Lord, too.

7

LEARNING TO READ
AND APPLY GOD'S WORD

My experience with godly counselors didn't end with a three-week stay at the Rapha center. That was the *start* of an ongoing counseling process that lasted for the next three years. The Rapha staff recommended counselors to me, and as I moved to various locations through the next three years, there always seemed to be a counselor available to me to help me continue in my journey to follow Jesus as the Lord of my life.

At the outset, I was meeting with a counselor twice a week, then once a week, then once a month, then once every two months. Along the way, I was learning more and more about how to read and *apply* God's Word to my everyday life and circumstances, to my marriage, and to my parenting.

Much of what I experienced in my new relationship with the Lord seemed like a spiritual confirmation of principles I had already learned through working with horses. That was true not only in my coming to Christ and receiving Jesus as my Savior, but also as I began to work forward in my life, trusting Jesus as Lord.

Step by step, and day by day, my new walk with the Lord took on a quality of TRAINING. I could see that I was being disciplined in a very straightforward and systematic way to trust God and to obey Him—at all times. He was in charge of the training. He was my "rider." Truly, I was experiencing a new form of "life in the saddle"—I was being directed by the Holy Spirit and helped by Him as I walked through new obstacles and situations.

That new path was and continues to be marked by three words: knowledge, understanding, and wisdom.

A Path of More
Knowledge

I discovered I was on a path that took me into more and more knowledge about God, about myself, and about how to know God and love other people.

The more I heard, read, and studied the Bible, and the more I grew in my ability to follow the leading of God's Holy Spirit, the more I grew in my knowledge about the way God does things, about how much God loves me and other people, and about God's desires for His children to change this world and increase the population of heaven.

I was confronted repeatedly by a new set of facts on which to base my life. First and foremost were the rock-solid absolute facts that I had been born anew, that God loved me, that He forgave me, and I was now in the process of being transformed and renewed by Him.

I began to learn that the character or nature of God was not what I had once thought it to be. I had grown up and continued to believe in my young adult life that God was a harsh judge, just waiting for me to slip up so He could punish me. I had a built-in anxiety about God that had led me to avoid Him whenever possible. I pretty much figured if I left God alone, He'd leave me alone.

I had to relearn the nature of God—which the Bible tells us is the exact same as the nature of Jesus. When I heard and read about Jesus, I saw Jesus as a person who was loving, gentle, kind, and patient with those who sincerely wanted Him and believed in Him. He was merciful, joyful, and trustworthy. He was forgiving, even if a person made multiple mistakes. He was the kind of person everybody would want as a close and loyal friend, confidant, and partner.

I had to learn that it was not GOD who sent sickness, obstacles, suffering, or other destructive calamities into my life. It was not GOD who sent things to me that were intended to result in my loss. Rather, it was the enemy of my soul who sent these things. God was the One who stood ready to help me and to turn me away from loss toward eternal gain. Jesus said it very clearly, "The thief [Jesus' name for the devil in this verse] comes only to steal and kill and destroy. I came that they may have life, and have it abundantly." (John 10:10 NAS)

- *Steal.* The devil comes to steal away anything that is good and helpful and beneficial. Jesus comes to GIVE what is good, helpful, and beneficial.

- *Kill.* The devil comes to kill our hopes, dreams, and the things we have accomplished for good. He comes ultimately to trap us into addictions and negative believing and eventually to kill us spiritually. Jesus comes to GIVE us hopes and dreams and things we are to do that will result in good for ourselves and other people. He comes to free us from addictions and negative attitudes and to give us an overflowing joy in life. Ultimately, the devil seeks to take us down with him into the pit of eternal death. Jesus ultimately seeks to GIVE us eternal life and everlasting purpose and joy.

- *Destroy.* The devil seeks to destroy our reputation, our integrity, and if we are married and have children, the devil seeks to destroy our marriage and our relationship with our children. He comes to destroy our ministry work, and in the end, to destroy our witness for Christ. He wants us to leave no lasting mark for good on this earth; he comes to destroy our legacy. Jesus comes to GIVE us His character, His ability to forge good relationships, and His call to win the lost and build up our fellow believers.

It is a very clear difference! The devil is the author of lies and death. To follow the devil is to follow a wide path that leads to total annihilation. Jesus is the source of all truth and life! To follow in His way is to walk a path that leads to everlasting paradise and reward, with blessings along the way.

A Path of More
Understanding

I began to discover that the more factual truths I learned about God, about myself, and about other people, the more I could begin to put those facts together for greater *understanding.* What I read in one part of God's Word became linked to what I read in another part of God's Word. I saw more and more examples of newly learned truths.

My increase in understanding also linked what I read in God's Word with what I knew to be true in my work with horses.

A person once said to me, "Tim, everything you read in the Bible seems hinged to something in your work with horses, and everything you know about horses seems to bring you right back to a truth in God's Word."

This isn't something I've worked at, as much as it is something I have allowed the Holy Spirit to do. It is God's Spirit, I believe, who gives me the insights I have had into how the world of horses and the Word of God are connected. It is God who has shown me certain concepts and principles, metaphors and analogies.

I am thoroughly convinced that God the Holy Spirit knows how to be the teacher of Tim O'Neal. He knows how to speak to my spirit in terms I understand, and to show me truth in a way that makes sense to me. He is the One who gave me a love for horses and an ability to work with them and show them. He is the One who has given me a love for His Word. He is the One who shows me that behind all things in the natural world are the things of the spiritual world.

The principles of the spiritual world are not in conflict with the natural world—rather, the spiritual world gives us insight into how better to manage and produce good things in the natural world.

The men who wrote the New Testament stated in a number of places that the purpose of the Law (the Old Testament law of Moses) was to show us our sinful nature as human beings, and to reveal the consequences of sin and rebellion, and to recognize our need for obedience and salvation. The Law was God's method for instructing His people to see the deadly danger of sin and turn to God's ways. The more the people knew the facts related to the Law and the history of God's people in following or rejecting the Law, the more the people grew in their *understanding*.

I see that as very similar to the way God seeks to train us as the people who are following Him as LORD. We are to learn not only what is right and wrong, but to see the consequences of choosing what is wrong and the benefits of choosing what is right. We are to understand the deeper *meaning* of life, and to see that the spiritual reality is the GREATER reality.

This world and this life—all that can be experienced by our sense of sight, sound, smell, taste, and touch—is temporary and fleeting. The spiritual realm is what truly lasts and is eternal. And furthermore, the spiritual life is intended by God to flow from the spiritual realm into the natural realm. It is intended to infuse and transform and bless all things in the natural realm.

None of us has a perfect understanding of this, but the good news of God's Word is that we can all *grow* in our understanding. We can all move beyond a knowledge of facts to a real understanding of God's plans and purposes. The fact that we *can* grow in our understanding is exciting to me! It gives a tremendous reason to get up every day and learn as much as we can learn about God's Word and about the relationship God desires for us to have with Him.

A Path of More
Wisdom

As we grow in understanding, we are to grow in wisdom, which is insight into the way God desires for us to APPLY what we are learning.

Every one of us has a different set of skills and abilities. We have different spiritual giftings and roles. We live in different areas, associate with different people, encounter different circumstances, and live different life spans in different cultures and traditions.

God has a plan and purpose for each person. It is a plan that involves worship of God, and serving or loving others. It is a unique plan that blends together all of our other unique traits.

Only God can be the author of the best plan for each person. And only God, through the work of the Holy Spirit in our lives, can give us the WISDOM about how to implement that plan for maximum results. God's WISDOM reveals who we are in His kingdom, what He wants us to do, how He wants us to enact His will, where and when He wants us to act, and with whom He wants us to work, play, and worship.

Wisdom leads us to make the right choices and decisions. It leads us to make the right affiliations and alliances, the right relationships, the right pursuit of the right opportunities.

Wisdom leads us to *want* more and more of the Holy Spirit at work in our lives so we might show more of God's love, joy, peace, patience, kindness, goodness, and trustworthiness to others.

Wisdom leads us to know deep within that God is in charge, of all things at all times, and that He is the Lord and we are His servants.

Wisdom leads us to awe about the majesty of God, who gives us a glorious opportunity to love and serve Him and truly make a difference for good in this world.

Our maturing into wisdom is a tremendous adventure! It is trusting God to put all of the jigsaw pieces of our life into a finished puzzle that reflects more of God to this world.

The path of knowledge, producing understanding, producing wisdom is a path that is a true joy to pursue. And, it is what following Jesus as LORD is all about.

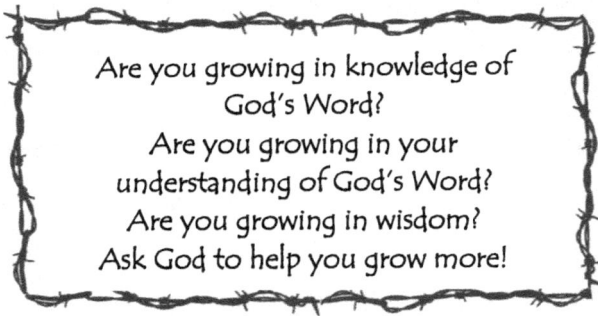

> Are you growing in knowledge of God's Word?
> Are you growing in your understanding of God's Word?
> Are you growing in wisdom?
> Ask God to help you grow more!

A Path for
All Believers

The path I've just described is a path for all who call Jesus Savior and Lord.

Someone once said to me, "Oh, Tim, you live your life the way you live it because you are the pastor of a church."

The truth is, I seek to live my life in accordance with God's Word *period.* It wouldn't matter if I were in business or another type of work. It doesn't matter that I train and show horses. The Word of God is the prescribed way for me to *live*. It is the standard for all my life choices, decisions, and my agenda and goals. I often say it this way:

The Word of God DEFINES my lifestyle.

The more I adopted this perspective and the more I began to *apply* the principles of God's Word to every area of my life, the more I saw real *changes*. In the past, I was prone to sizing up circumstances and situations with my rational mind, and then determining the course of action to take. In many ways, I had allowed the world around me to define my actions, and my subsequent attitudes and decisions. As I allowed the Word of God to define me, I began to see the world around me change as I changed.

This isn't just because of ME, Tim O'Neal. This is the pattern that occurs with all believers in Christ Jesus who truly are trusting God to guide them with His Word. It is what happens when people who know and are applying God's Word walk into any room. The atmosphere of the room changes—and the amazing thing is that the people in the room aren't even aware consciously of the change! The level of anger nearly always drops. The use of profanity and the telling of dirty jokes seem to stop. The people in the room deal with one another in a little more courteous or polite way. In many cases, there is increased cooperation and a more positive way of looking at problems and their solutions.

My Increased
Frustration

Through those years of counseling, I certainly developed an increasing hunger to know the Word of God . . . more and more and more. We began going to churches where we could count on the Word of God being preached. I developed an almost insatiable hunger to know the Word of God and to see *how*—when and in what ways—I might apply its truth to my daily life.

With this increased hunger came an increased frustration. My two main frustrations were these:

First, I am a slow reader. I can read the words on the page as quickly as most people. But when it comes to comprehending what I read and remembering it, that's another story. All through school, I struggled with reading comprehension, which a teacher once explained to me is a combination of understanding what is written and having an ability to remember the meaning and use it later. If you *show* me how to do something, I probably will never forget it. If you tell me something verbally and I'm paying attention to what you are saying, I won't forget it. If I have my choice, I'll ask you to show me how to do something and then let me try to do it myself. When that happens, I most certainly won't forget it and I'll be able to do it better and better and even teach others how to do it. Those in the education field would tell you that I am a "kinetic" learner—I learn by doing.

I have learned through the years that discouragement very often arises because we aren't seeing the *results* we want *as quickly as we want to see them.* We live in a world that seeks instant gratification. We may *like* a slow-cooked meal, but few of us these days want to cook a meal that takes time to prepare.

I wanted a faster intake of knowledge, a faster depth of understanding, a faster development of wisdom!

There was no doubt that I wanted to DO the Word of God. That became and remains the focus of my desire! But for me to *do* the Word, I first had to learn it. And the process of reading the Word to learn it seemed painfully slow to me.

I certainly understand that we are saved by grace through faith. (See Ephesians 2:8.) We are not saved by "learning," or by any other work. However, we are challenged by the Lord to learn to apply God's Word to our lives. *Applying* is a *learning* process.

My second frustration had to do with the fact that I am easily distracted unless something is supremely interesting to me. Fortunately, horses and my family members are supremely interesting! I can get bored very easily and let my mind wander, or let my eyes wander, and the end result of that is that I begin to see all sorts of things around me that are more interesting than what a person is telling me. That was a major difficulty in school. What the other students were doing, what was happening outside the classroom windows, or even what I could *imagine* . . . all these things were far more interesting than listening to a teacher give a lecture or present homework instructions. I wanted to learn the Bible, but in truth, I wanted a personal tutor to help me—not a systematic course or method that required a daily focus on a curriculum.

I complained to Gypsy about it more than once. I'd say, "I wish somebody could just come and sit across the dining table from me and teach me the Bible." Or I'd say, "I wish somebody could just open up my skull and pour the Word of God into it." I wanted to learn, but the learning process of reading and studying on my own was painful and slow. It tried my patience, which I still didn't have much of.

Gypsy's simple, straightforward response to my complaints was, "Maybe God is leading you to go to Bible school."

No way. Go to *school?* That had all sorts of negativity associated with it in my mind. I wanted nothing to do with lectures and exams and passing courses. I just wanted to *know* the Bible, not be in a disciplined and strict environment for *learning* it.

So I'd complain some more, and each time, Gypsy would say, "Sounds to me as if you are supposed to go to Bible school."

When my protests didn't work, she finally said, "If you don't want to go to Bible school, how would you feel about *my* going to Bible school?" That was another matter entirely. I wasn't at all opposed to her going to Bible school. In fact, if truth were known, that seemed like a possible solution for *me.* She could learn what the teachers had to say and tell me about it over dinner. I'd never need to set foot in a classroom to get the same benefit.

Gypsy began to research various Bible schools and she discovered that there were a number of very highly recommended ones associated with churches in the area of Tulsa, Oklahoma. We explored those options and finally decided that Gypsy would go to Victory Christian Center's Bible training institute. We sold out and moved to Tulsa.

And once we got there, it became apparent that I was also *supposed* to go to Bible school.

8

EMBRACING MY NEW IDENTITY IN CHRIST JESUS

I will never forget my first day of orientation at Victory Bible Institute. I sat on the front row—I knew from my past that this was the best place for a person with attention deficit disorder to sit. There were fewer distractions. All of my focus could be on the speaker. And there I sat, hearing the speaker tell us that as future Victory Bible Institute students, we were expected to look and act in the most professional manner possible. Then he added, "No cowboy boots and belt buckles, like you just came in off the ranch. Dress like the professional minister you are training to be."

Well, there I sat wearing cowboy boots and a large belt buckle that proclaimed I had won a major world championship in the horse-show world! I didn't own a pair of shoes that weren't boots. I was proud of my accomplishments and that particular belt buckle was a sign to others that I was a success. It reflected my identity as a top horseman and trainer!

We left that meeting, and as we were driving, I said to Gypsy, "What do you think about what that guy said about cowboy boots and belt buckles?" She replied, "It sounds to me like you have a problem with it. Is it possible that you have your identity wrapped up in those boots and buckle?"

We both knew that this man had not singled me out. He was speaking in general terms. Nevertheless, I was the only one in the room who fit his description of a person who wasn't dressed properly for Bible school training. I wanted to fit in and even more than that, I wanted to be obedient to whatever God might be asking me to change in my life. A new belt and pair of shoes seemed to be a step of obedience I needed to take.

We went straight to a store where I spent ninety-seven dollars on a new dress belt and a pair of dress shoes. This was a major investment for us. I only had a hundred dollars in my pocket, and when we walked out of that store, I only had three dollars to my name. Fortunately, I had gas in our vehicle to get me to where we were to have dinner with a longstanding friend, and I knew that he had invited us to dinner so he likely was going to pay for dinner. I certainly was counting on that.

When we had finished our excellent meal with this man, he asked me something that I wasn't at all expecting. He asked me if I would be willing to ride, and train, a horse that he had purchased. He told me that he considered this a *job*, not a favor, and he then handed me a hundred-dollar bill and said, "This is my first payment to you to get started on this."

I could hardly believe what was happening, but both Gypsy and I took this as a wonderful sign of God's blessing on the decision I had made. We had a deep belief that God not only *would* take care of us financially as we went to Bible school, but He was already taking care of us!

My championship belt buckle was no longer going to be my *identity*. My identity was going to be first and foremost the identity of a person committed to doing whatever kind of ministry God called me to. I suspected that I would still be riding horses—and yes, training horses and showing horses. But my real IDENTITY changed that day in a tangible, lasting way.

I still enjoy working with horses and training horses, but my number-one goal in life changed during those Bible school days. I no longer have goals related to my teaching people how to train or show horses. My foremost goal is to share the insights I have had spiritually as the result of my working with horses and my reading and applying the Word of God to my life.

Every horse trainer who *teaches* others about horse training has his or her own method and approach, and all sorts of reasons why their method and approach is the best. I don't know if my horse-training methods are the best for everybody. They have worked for *me*. But teaching these methods is not my aim in life. My aim is to help people grow spiritually and to come to a dynamic, full, and meaningful relationship with Jesus as their Savior and Lord. Period.

The Lord has given me literally hundreds of insights into how the Word of God and my experiences with horses line up, like parallels—the horse experiences are a metaphor in the natural world for what God's Word teaches. My experiences in the show-horse world are an example of the way God works in the spiritual realm to train *us* to be His prized people.

People talk about "horse whisperers." I don't aspire to be known that way. My goal is to present GOD as the One who whispers into the heart of a man or woman to speak His love and His plan and purpose for their life.

> God is the One who whispers into
> the heart of a man or woman to
> speak His love and His plan and purpose
> for their life.

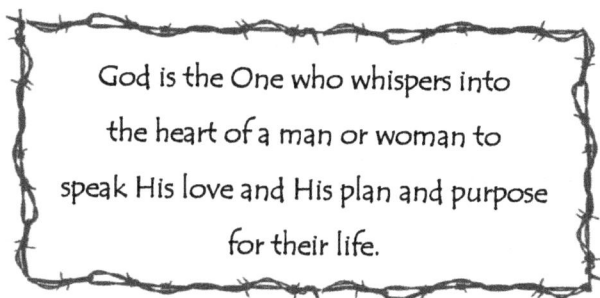

I also do not see myself as a horse trainer or horse showman who occasionally gives a word of witness about Jesus. Rather, I am a minister of the Gospel, and now the pastor of a church since 1998, who has opportunities from time to time to preach from the back of a horse.

After two years of Bible school, attending Bible classes with Gypsy for four hours a day, five days a week, I came to a realization that my future was to be in the ministry to some degree. That had not been my motivation for going to Bible school, but it became the direction for my life as I went to Bible school. I had been trained at VBI to listen to God, and more and more, I wanted to know what HE wanted me to say and do, and how to apply His Word.

I discovered that I never got tired of learning God's Word. In fact, the more I learned, the more I wanted to learn! That was a new experience for me. Learning God's Word was a joy, and learning how to apply God's Word was even greater joy.

One day as I was riding home from a veterinary appointment, I had a vision of myself riding around in an arena talking to people about Jesus from the back of a horse.

Well, those days are now here. I am speaking more and more from the back of a horse . . . and I'm loving every opportunity to do that!

I have a very clear understanding today that I am to be a *minister* who reaches out to people with the Gospel message, through the horses. I spend many hours every year in counseling people from the horse world who call or come to visit with me about how they might experience the peace and purpose I have found in Christ Jesus.

I am a *minister* who loves horses—that has never changed—but who sees what happens in the process of training and showing a horse as having a parallel meaning to how God trains us to be His disciples as we prepare for an eternity with Him.

My self-worth once was based upon the performances of the horses I rode. Their accomplishments became *my* accomplishments. Their winnings gave me value.

My self-identity today is based upon my relationship with Christ Jesus!

9

LEARNING TO TRUST THE
LORD IN ALL THINGS

The Word of God says, "Seek first the kingdom of
God and His righteousness, and all these things [that you
need in life] shall be added to you." (See Matthew 6:33.)

As I began to absorb the Word of God—learning it,
understanding it, applying its wisdom to my life—I began to
see that the Word of God had very specific meaning to me
and to my needs on any given day. The Word of God gave
Tim O'Neal direction about *how* I was to trust God for
particular circumstances, problems, or in specific
relationships.

DOC EBONEE

The things that I need are likely to be *some* of the same things that you and every other person need. But there are also going to be some things in my life that are NOT the same. I may not have a need you have; and you may not have needs that I presently have. The Word of God says that ALL the things we need are provided for us by the Lord. That's the promise of His Word.

One of the things that every person needs—and it is a good place to begin every day—is to have a "quiet mind."

Developing a
Quiet Mind

One of the major signs of a mature Christian is the ability to be so in tune with the Holy Spirit, and so sensitive to His directives, that we adjust our approach to problems, and our actions within difficult relationships and situations, to be in complete accord with the Spirit's *leading*. We must come to the place where we are moving spiritually in total sync with His desires, plans, and purposes. We are quiet in our spirits. We have no jagged or abrupt behaviors—rather, we are in the "flow" that He has designed for us.

This doesn't happen quickly or easily. It is the result of a great deal of time and increased sensitivity spent in *how* we listen to the Lord and how we trust Him in all things. It is a result of our applying God's Word in hundreds of ways in hundreds of circumstances. It is what it means to become "one" with the Lord, which is something He promised to His disciples when He prayed for them, "Keep through Your name those whom You have given Me, that they may be one as We are." (John 17:11)

To a great extent, I learned through the horses the advantages of developing a truly QUIET mind.

Horses are flighty animals, easily spooked. A horse that has been well trained and is disciplined is often referred to as a "quiet" horse. The quiet horse is one that is submissive to its trainer, and listens to what its rider commands—verbally or with hand or leg cues, or shifts of the rider's body in the saddle, and is quick to respond in a smooth even manner.

If a horse becomes fearful or overly nervous, its first instinct is to run, and if there's no room to run, it will kick. A horse that senses danger—real or merely perceived—will turn its head nervously, looking for the danger and also the way out of it.

A quiet horse, in contrast, is a horse that may register anxiety in its eyes, but won't turn its head. It stands still.

If there is a big noise—a large clap, as an example, or if something unexpected blows across its path, the quiet horse will continue to move forward without a sudden stop or thought of fleeing.

A quiet horse is an enjoyable horse to ride. It has already learned what a rider wants, and therefore, it doesn't need to be told every second of a ride what to do.

A horse that is *not* quiet is usually called a "busy-minded" horse. This can be the result of many factors. The horse may have too much mental energy, often caused by its spending too much time in a stall and not enough physical activity or variety of experience. The horse may not have been exposed to enough circumstances, which results in the horse seeing everything in its world as if for the first time—which can create anxiety. The horse might also be of a temperament that makes it more curious or more eager to exert its own will.

A busy-minded horse may be that way naturally, or it may have become that way because of an erratic rider, trainer, or owner.

A busy-minded horse does not learn as quickly as a quiet horse. It is easily distracted, which means that it generally takes more repetitions of a drill or sequence for the horse to learn what is being asked of it. This is much like a person who has attention deficit disorder— that person tends to take longer to learn something because he or she is easily distracted and the learning process seems continually to be interrupted.

A busy-minded horse is not focused on its trainer or rider. It is not listening *only* to its rider. A chirping bird or a dog running in the pasture is going to capture its interest, to the detriment of the training process.

What a picture of some of us! A person can get caught up in fear, "drama," or negative circumstances. We can become distracted by things great and small. And the net result is that we get our eyes off the Lord, we stop listening with full focus to the inner voice of the Holy Spirit, and we feel stress because our minds are literally moving in a dozen directions at the same time.

As a person who has ADHD (attention deficit hyperactivity disorder), I know how difficult it is to maintain focus in my life, and also how *important* it is to do so! I know very well the meaning of what the apostle Paul wrote when he said that we must take every thought captive. As I approach each new circumstance in my life, I must consciously and intentionally ask myself, "What does the Word of God say about this situation?" I must focus my mind on God's Word, and once I have determined what it is the Word of God teaches on that particular issue, I must then say, "Now how am I going to apply the Word?" Once I begin to apply the Word—in what I say and the actions that I take—there's something about the speaking or doing that engages my mind more fully and I can proceed with focus.

Knowing that I am acting in accordance with the Word of God gives me peace. A focused person tends to be a peaceful person—*and* be a person with a quiet spirit or a quiet mind. I get more done, and that, in itself, is both rewarding and motivating.

Are you busy minded

or

quiet minded?

Getting God's Priorities
for the Day Ahead

The command to seek FIRST the kingdom of God—in other words, to seek God's commands, God's promises, God's methods, God's purposes, and God's protocols—is the same command to all people. But again, in all likelihood, we are going to be convicted by the Holy Spirit that there is one or perhaps two or three *specific* acts of seeking that we are to do individually and personally. I may feel a conviction to read a particular passage of the Bible; you may be convicted to spend a quiet time before the Lord in thanksgiving, praise, and intercession. I may feel a conviction to reprioritize my list of things to do that day; you may feel a conviction to call a particular person to apologize for something you know has hurt that person.

The truth is, God has something for you to do . . . every day. He has a plan and purpose for your life. Finding those specific things God has for you is an adventure—it is a process of discovery!

Knowledge PLUS. The Word of God tells us that the devil has a tremendous "knowledge" of God—of Jesus, of God's plans and purposes, God's commandments, and so forth. But he doesn't apply any of the knowledge of God to his existence. When you begin to apply the Word of God, you gain knowledge *PLUS.* You begin to learn how to trust the Holy Spirit to *help* you in your daily walk.

Many people have read the Bible and have a basic "knowledge" of what it says, at least in some books and chapters. But they don't apply what it says to their lives. They *live* according to their own impulses and lusts, or according to what others around them say, or what the culture as a whole tells them. As a result, they don't truly live in the freedom that God desires for them.

Any person can be set free from sin and bondage to it. Any person can know the assurance of eternal life. Any person can put himself into a position to receive the abundant life that Jesus promised. But for a person to receive all that, he or she must choose to *apply* God's Word personally and seek to think, see, speak, and act in the way the Bible teaches. There must be knowledge, certainly. But beyond knowledge, there must be a commitment to *doing* what the Bible says. Daily. In every circumstance of life. In every relationship. For as long as a person walks this earth.

We must believe that Jesus is the resurrected Son of God and that He sent the Holy Spirit to us to guide us continually. But then, we must *ask* the Holy Spirit to do His work in us, through us, and all around us. We must *invite* the Spirit—which is an act of our will—to reveal Himself to us and to show us all of the rewards that God desires for us.

Right here are several things that God wants as your priorities for *today:*

- To live in a greater awareness that Jesus has sent the Holy Spirit to help you apply the Word of God and resist all temptation to sin.
- To pursue those things that put you in a position to receive the abundant life God's Word promises you. (See John 10:10.)
- To begin to *see* yourself applying the Word of God.

And there's more!

Learning to Think in New Ways. When we read the Word of God, the Word stimulates our mind so that we think the way God thinks. God is our Creator, and He continues to create every day. Reading and applying the Word of God stimulates our creativity so we begin to put into place new and beneficial things that are for good in this world.

The Word of God also stimulates our emotions so that we begin to forgive others, encourage others, and do our best to show compassion to others. And, it stimulates our desire to know God better. The more we know the Word of God, the more we *want* to know the Word. And, the more we want to know the Author of the Word. We grow in our desire to know the risen Christ and to learn how to relate to the Holy Spirit. The good news is that the Word of God and the presence of God NEVER disappoint. They always satisfy. They always renew and refresh us, and give us a tremendous inner peace and sense of fulfillment.

- Are you expecting and receiving new, innovative, creative ideas from God? You can!
- Are you seeing a need to love others in new ways . . . and to have greater compassion for others?

- Are you more willing to forgive others, and perhaps to go to a specific person to ask forgiveness?
- Are you a quick source of encouragement to others?

All of these are things that God desires for us to do *on a daily basis.*

Applying God's Word
Gives Great Purpose

Applying God's Word gives great purpose to any day! It gives direction, and, as a person does what he or she knows to do, there is a satisfaction that the person has obeyed God and contributed something to this world that God desires. There's a tremendous fulfillment that comes when you know that you have been a blessing to others, and are growing personally in your relationship with the Lord at the same time.

When I break colts I put them in a round pen. The ideal situation is for the horse and me to build a relationship in which the horse *trusts* me. I want the horse to come to the place where it wants to stand in the center of the pen with me. But initially, the colt is afraid of me, and it runs in the only direction and path provided for it—at the outer edge of the round pen, running round and round, trying to escape what it cannot truly escape. A colt that is allowed to run as long as it wants to run is a colt that can run to the point of making itself dehydrated and sick, even to the point of death.

Ideally, I would like for the colt to stop running, face up to me and want to come to me, where we can build our relationship on trust. I do not want to force him; instead I want to position myself in a way that will draw the horse to me. I want the horse to quit running in fear, and begin to listen to and have faith in me, to realize I want to guide and direct him to make the right choices in life. I give him the opportunity to make choices while I am working him in the round pen. The horse can choose to turn toward me or away from me, to run from me or stop and come to me. I continue to make the right choice easy for him and the wrong choice difficult. Every move I make is to encourage the horse to listen to me, instead of running from me. The greatest lesson the horse and I can both learn is:

Listen to learn and learn to listen.

I know that I was once like an unbroken colt. So was every other genuine believer in Christ Jesus that I have come to know over the years.

I was running in circles, trying to avoid submission to the One who desired only good for me. I wore myself out in my running, doing what I wanted to do and enjoying what I thought I was enjoying (which I wasn't *really* enjoying, but didn't know it). Going to the Rapha clinic for help was my point of stopping, and eventually turning to the One who could train me to have purpose and deep meaning in life.

If you are in that position today, I encourage you to stop running in circles. Develop a quiet mind. Put your focus on God's Word. Read it and ask the Holy Spirit to show you how to apply it. And then, begin to walk with purpose. Trust the Holy Spirit to lead you, to provide for you, and to show you what He has for you to accomplish *today*.

God's Word Frees
a Person from Fear

A cycle of GOOD is developed the more we read and apply God's Word. First and foremost, we see that God's Word *works*. We discover that God will lead us to do things that make a positive and beneficial impact, not only in our life but in the lives of others. We experience joy when we apply God's Word and see those good results.

We also grow in our trust of the Lord. When God asks us to do something that seems difficult, perhaps even impossible to us, we are willing to take the risk—He has been faithful in the past, and we have no reason to conclude that He will be anything other than faithful today.

Our faith *in* God develops into trust *of* God.

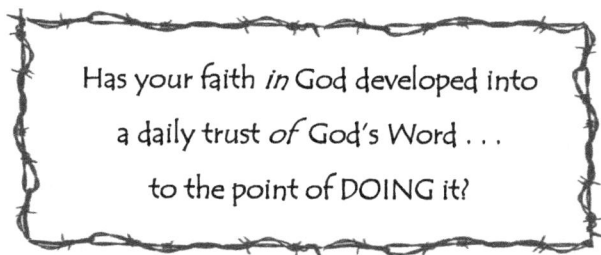

Has your faith *in* God developed into a daily trust *of* God's Word . . . to the point of DOING it?

Trust always comes as a result of spending time, over time. It comes spiritually, by spending time with the Lord—not just a few seconds here and there, not just for a few minutes on a Sunday. It comes from being aware that you are walking with the Lord throughout every day, and you are walking and talking with Him often, and sometimes, for long conversations.

Trust of another person comes as you spend quality time with that person.

In the horse world, a person must spend considerable time with a horse for that horse truly to *trust*. It takes time for a trainer to *learn* the basic instincts and tendencies of a horse. It takes time for the horse to *learn* how a person sits in a saddle, and what various cues mean when it comes to the behavior the trainer desires from the horse. The process of building trust takes hours, days, weeks, and months. A few hours on a single day is not going to be sufficient for building trust. Spending a quality amount of time, *over time*, is what results in trust.

When I was a boy, some of the neighbor boys, as well as my brother, built a certain degree of fear in me about going outside after dark. Inevitably, it seemed, I'd go out—perhaps to take out the trash—and one or more of these older boys would hide in the bushes and then jump out to scare me, or they would make strange noises in the deep shadows of the foliage around our house, and these strange noises were terrifying to me.

As an adult, I don't live with that fear, but I also readily admit that when I go outside at night, my ears are on high alert for strange sounds, and I am looking into the shadows for any sign of danger. Where I live in rural Kansas, a person can never be sure that a coyote or fox isn't lurking in the darkness.

The foremost way I have found to combat this type of fear, and other fears, is to begin thanking the Lord for His presence at all times, and in all circumstances. I don't thank the Lord *for* the frightening or worrisome situation. Rather, I thank the Lord *in* the situation, and above all I thank Him for His steady, calming, trustworthy presence.

The Lord is the Lord *all the time*. He doesn't act one way on a given day and then another way the next day. His character is always true to His Word, His judgments are always sure, His commandments are always in full effect, and His love is without measure or end. The Lord can be *counted on* to be who He says He is in the Word of God.

I can *trust* the Lord for walking with me *through* all situations and circumstances. My knowing that the Word of God is always trustworthy allows me to live daily through a wide variety of difficulties and troubling events with confidence, boldness, and comfort. *Trust* allows me to live with peace in my heart and mind.

Making a *decision* to trust happened in a day, but learning what *it fully meant* to trust occurred over time in my life—years, even decades, to get to the place where I am at today.

I did not grow up with a lot of Bible teaching or church attendance. The bad part of that was that I didn't have the opportunity to know God in a personal way or develop a relationship with Him from my earliest years. But the *good* part in not growing up in the church was that I didn't develop any false church-taught conclusions about God's nature or negative conclusions about how God desired to relate to me. In coming to know the Lord in a personal way when I did, and then a few years later going to Bible school, I had the benefit of being taught the Word of God by stable, mature Christian leaders who were trusting God and trusting the Word of God *fully*, applying the Word to every circumstance in their daily lives. They modeled trust for me.

Doubt and fear and worry all come back to the central issue of trust.

If you are struggling with doubt, fear, or anxiety, the cure for all of that is a deeper relationship with the Lord. In learning to trust Him, and in carrying out His plan for you on a daily basis—as you read and apply the Word of God—you will find doubts, fears, and worries leaving your life.

The Role of
Communication

Trust is a process that involves consistent communication, and frequent communication.

I don't recommend any particular method when it comes to talking to God. The point is this: *Talk to Him!* Tell Him how you feel, what is going on in your life, and what you are struggling with. Thank Him for the ways He has helped you and provided for you in the past. He has already helped you by Jesus dying on the cross! Realize what He has already done for you—and thank Him for that! Praise Him because you know that He not only *can* help you, but also *wants* to help you. Ask Him for His help.

And above all, *listen* to what God says back to you. Listening is the biggest part of communication. As a person once said, "God gave you one mouth and two ears. We should listen twice as much as we talk." That's good advice for every person, in most relationships, most of the time!

Most of the time, the way we listen to God is to read His Word with a quiet mind, looking for God to speak to us.

The Word of God says this about itself: It is *inspired.* That means it is God-breathed, written for mankind as the Holy Spirit inspired those who wrote it. Therefore, when a person makes a decision to *do* what the Bible says, that person *is* following the leading and guidance of the Holy Spirit.

The Holy Spirit Convicts. The more we develop an ongoing daily relationship with the Holy Spirit, the more the HOLY SPIRIT nudges us. He never nags us. But He does convict us as part of guiding us.

The Holy Spirit whispers in my heart and the heart of every willing believer in Christ, "Are you doing what the Word tells you to do? Are you applying the Word to this particular circumstance that is troubling to you? Are you asking the right questions of the Word and are you looking for God's answers? Are you walking in the fullness of the revelation knowledge you have been given?"

Think about it. The Lord may be asking you as He has asked me from time to time:

"Tim, are you trusting Me for mercy?"

"Tim, are you applying that truth from God's Word in a consistent way in all your relationships?"

"Tim, are you spending as much time in the Word as you should spend?"

The truth is that I *want* to do what God wants me to do. I want to trust Him more and more. I want to be more and more consistent. I want to know more and more of His Word. And I also know that I need more and more of the Holy Spirit's help to enable and empower me to DO what I want to do in Him!

There's no way to get to that point without persevering or enduring. We must NOT give up. We must NOT seek shortcuts. We must NOT become disillusioned or discouraged.

Rather, we must put forth the active effort to continue on with Christ Jesus. We must put forth the active effort to learn more and more of God's Word and be open to more and more ways of applying it to our daily lives.

Revelation Knowledge. The Holy Spirit also opens up the Word of God to us in ways that give us new insights and new inspiration. This is known as "revelation knowledge." The deep meanings of the Word of God are revealed to us with greater impact and with a motivation to take action.

Revelation knowledge is knowledge that is being revealed to your spirit with a firm conviction: *This is what God wants for ME.* This is how God desires for ME to think, to see, to speak, and to act. This is the direction God wants ME to walk in.

The revelation is poured out to all people in the Word. But the revelation is not *perceived,* or received, by all people. Many people read the Word like a textbook and even before they lay down the Book, they have forgotten what they read. That's usually because they weren't reading it for its meaning and application. They were only reading it because they thought Bible reading was a good thing to do, or they were reading it for mere information. There's a big difference when you open the Word of God with a prayerful desire: "Show me, Lord, how You want to change me by what I am reading."

Go to God's Word with the idea in mind that you *are* going to be challenged to change.

The Rewards of
Peace and Consistency

A life of trust in the Lord, and of purpose in applying His Word, produces a life that is not only peaceful, but also consistent.

Looking back, my early adult years were anything but consistent and peaceful. I was in turmoil on the inside, and constantly racing from one thing to the next on the outside. Life today is far more consistent, and that does not at all mean boring. Every day is a challenge—not because I'm in frantic search of challenge, but because God sets before me the challenges He wants me to pursue and that *He will help me accomplish.* I have a deep awareness in advance of taking on a challenge that I'm going to succeed at it, because God is the One who is directing my steps, leading the way, and working in me and through me.

I have a tremendous peace as the result of the way I live my life, applying God's Word to every aspect of it. I have a confidence that this is what God desires for me, and that His rewards and blessings flow toward me because I trust Him to lead and guide my every move. There's nothing "special" about Tim O'Neal. I am thoroughly convinced that this is the lifestyle that God desires for *every person.*

Trusting God is not just a great way to live . . . it is the *greatest* way to live!

Furthermore, a life of trusting God is a life of constantly moving *forward*. Fear, doubt, and worry can cause a person to get stuck—very often in a reality that is unpleasant or negative. Fear keeps a person from doing what God desires, and therefore, from receiving all that God desires to give.

If a person is afraid to use his talents and gifts, there are many things in life that are left "undone," and the person will simultaneously experience a deep longing and feeling of dissatisfaction. A person who is bottled up by fear cannot live up to his full potential or purpose. And it is only as we trust God to help us reach our potential and purpose that we have deep meaning for our lives.

Fear can keep a person from opening up their life to love and to vulnerable communication and intimacy with others. This is true in the human world and the horse world. It is true in a person's relationship with God. To truly *feel* God's love and approval, a person *must* come to the place of trust in God. It is then that a person is *abiding* in the Lord. It is then that God becomes more real. And it is in abiding that we become more fruitful, more useful, and more fulfilled.

10

SPEAKING THE WORD OF GOD

Even people who don't know very much about horses tend to know that a "bit" can be put into a horse's mouth—the bit is a metal mouthpiece that is connected to a headpiece and reins. Taken together, the headpiece, bit, and reins are called a "bridle."

The bit in the horse's mouth is what a rider uses to direct the movements of a horse. The bit is vital in telling the horse which direction to turn and how quickly, and how quickly to stop or slow down.

The bit *guides* the horse, in ways that are practical . . . but also in a way that is mostly unseen to the outside world.

Those who are in the horse world know that bits come in many different styles and types that have been developed to be used in a variety of ways for different purposes. A bit must *fit* the horse, and also fit the tasks that a rider is going to ask the horse to do.

A bit will cause a horse to carry its head, neck, and body in a unique way.

I have trained horses using one kind of bit, and then used another kind of bit for showing.

Different verses and passages in the Bible do the same in us. The Word causes us to carry ourselves in the world in a unique way. And, there are some verses and passages that the Lord speaks to us in the privacy of His training and disciplining us, and other verses and passages are ones that He expects us to teach, preach, or speak to other people in a public way.

Some bits keep a horse under better control, actually keeping a horse more focused and less distracted.

There are literally hundreds of types of bits. At a large horse show, you are going to find many types of bits being used, by different breeds of horses in different classes of competition, by horses and riders of unique temperament. You are also likely to find the same style or "make and model" of bit being used by more than one horse—even though those horses are competing in different events.

Are you aware that the Bible has a specific passage about bits? The Word of God says: "We all stumble in many things. If anyone does not stumble in word, he is a perfect man, able also to bridle the whole body. Indeed, we put bits in horses' mouths that they may obey us, and we turn their whole body." (See James 3:2–3.) The writer of this passage goes on to point out that our tongue is a "little member" of the body, but the tongue can become a devastating fire, or a source of blessings. (See James 3:5–12.)

As followers of Jesus, our Lord, we each have a unique purpose for our lives, and in any given day, we each have a set of distinctive tasks that the Lord desires for us to do in fulfilling that purpose.

The Word of God Is
the "Bit" that Guides Us

What is our "bit"—the means by which we are guided? It is the Word of God!

When we put the Word of God into our mouths, that Word will control what we do, how we do it, and when and where we do it. It will set into motion our actions and our conversations.

A particular word in one person's mouth may control that person in one area of their life, and not have the same effect in another person's life. But a particular word in that other person's mouth may control or direct their actions in a way that isn't readily obvious to me.

This does not mean that God's Word is *different* for every person. Rather, it means that every *person* is different and God's Word still fits each person and produces godly thoughts, words, and actions in that person's life. God's Word is universal—in that it applies to everybody on the planet. God's Word is also highly individualized—God has a particular application for everything He speaks to us directly by the Holy Spirit or through the written Bible to guide us, lead us, direct us, and help us succeed in the plans and purposes designed for us.

Let me share with you three specific things that the Word is intended to do in our lives, and through our lives to touch the lives of others.

The Word Is Intended
to Edify—or Build Up

God's Word tells me that I am to speak *only* what edifies, or "builds up." (See Ephesians 4:29.) Since I am the first person who is going to hear what comes out of my own mouth, the foremost person I am going to edify in my life is Tim O'Neal!

The opposite of "edify," of course, is to demean or to destroy. What we say also has the power to destroy, both others and ourselves.

What I choose to say, therefore, is critically important to my attitude, the development of my own character, and my preparation to be a suitable vessel for the Lord to use in ministering to other people.

In an earlier chapter I indicated that prior to the time I accepted Jesus as my Savior and Lord, I had a very foul mouth. Not only did I speak words that were curse words and "dirty" words, I also prided myself on my ability to "cut down" other people through skillfully wielded words of sarcasm and cynicism. I rarely, if ever, had anything GOOD to say. My language was negative, demeaning, critical, and destructive.

While I was delivered of my physical addictions at the time of my accepting Christ, and while I was transformed in my spirit, I struggled in an ongoing way to change my vocabulary and my cynical and sarcastic attitude.

One day in my reading and studying of God's Word, I came across the verse that says, "Let no corrupt word proceed out of your mouth, but what is good for necessary edification, that it may impart grace to the hearers."

(Ephesians 4:29) Grace is the work of God. In other words, I must not speak any word that would hinder a person from experiencing the work of God in their life—or in my life.

The Holy Spirit immediately convicted me that I needed to clean up my communication. God's Word was not, and is not, a "suggestion." This was a direct command in the Word of God. I needed to obey it.

I said to Gypsy, "We are no longer going to use any foul or destructive language in our home. We are going to speak *only* what builds up, not what tears down. We are *not* going to have sarcasm and cynicism spoken in our home. We are not going to use words to ridicule or criticize. We are going to be a family that speaks positive, godly, uplifting words to one another."

Gypsy agreed with me that this was a good standard to establish in our family, but as Gypsy also has said on a number of occasions, "Things got real quiet at our house." For almost three months, there was very little spoken within the walls of our home. None of us could think of anything positive, godly, or uplifting to say!

Gradually, however, we learned to change our vocabulary and our attitudes to produce only messages that were good for the building up of character and integrity—for us as individual family members, and as words of encouragement one to the other. It was a dramatic change, not only in our dinnertime conversation, but also in our relationships as family members. When you seek to build up a person, that person is going to feel more valued, with healthier self-worth, and the person is going to be more prone to valuing others. There is a flow of genuine love that comes from edification!

I can still get into sarcasm and cynicism if I am not careful. Daily, I must allow God's Word to wash my mind, and also to wash my language. I must actively and intentionally speak what edifies.

What about a person who has not had a tendency to be sarcastic, critical, or to put down others verbally? The same Word of God, the very same verse, may serve a slightly different function in their mouth. That verse in Ephesians may be a direct word of guidance to refrain from telling falsehoods—even "little white lies." It might be a direct word of guidance to refrain from spreading rumors or gossiping. It might be a direct word of guidance to refrain from speaking what has been told in confidence, or to refrain from something that another person might think is slander. The words associated with falsehoods, gossip, slander, and breaking of confidence are just as "corrupt" as swearing, telling dirty jokes, or engaging in sarcasm, criticism, and put-downs.

The Word of God is unchanging. The mouths from which the Word of God is spoken are different—the people who speak it have different issues, and different lessons to be learned from the Lord. At all times, however, the Word of God is to become our guide for *what* to say, and how to speak to others.

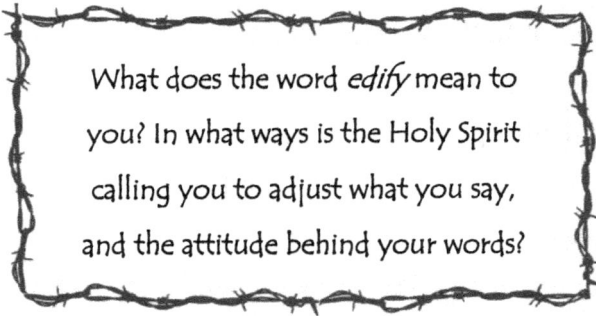

> What does the word *edify* mean to you? In what ways is the Holy Spirit calling you to adjust what you say, and the attitude behind your words?

The Word of God Is Intended to Produce Wise Counsel

The Word of God is knowledge to our minds. It leads us to understanding. It creates an opportunity for wisdom to develop as we apply the Word. But the Word of God does not give us specific factual details about everything we might face in a day. It doesn't tell us, for example, which stocks to purchase on the stock market, or where to find the best price for the new appliance we need, or how to find the best surgeon for our medical problem. Rather, the Word of God creates in us a mindset that helps us evaluate advice and information that comes our way.

The Holy Spirit gives us "discernment" as we take in information or seek information.

Early in my desire to follow Jesus as my Lord, I made a decision that I was not going to watch—on television, DVDs, or movies—anything that presented a lifestyle I didn't want to live. In plain language, I wasn't going to watch anything that used language I didn't want to speak, or engage in sins I didn't want to commit, or have committed against me. I felt a very strong conviction that I needed to say NO to most of what the media wanted to dump into my mind.

Let me give you an example. I do not want to cheat other people. I want to live an honest, straightforward, trustworthy life. The Bible calls me to that standard. I want to follow that standard.

But what does our culture tell us, in large doses? That cheating is not only acceptable, but also desirable—just as long as you don't get caught, and as long as you don't hurt other people "too much." People who live with a continual desire to cheat others—or who are always in pursuit of ill-gotten gain, or who are trying to justify a life of sinful relationships, are all around us, seemingly all of the time.

Come on, now—don't try to tell me that this isn't at the core of MOST prime-time dramatic and comedy shows, and don't try to tell me that a significant percentage of our population doesn't have these desires at the core of its daily behavior.

How many episodes of the comedy most Americans have seen are based on storylines that involve cheating, drinking to excess, or lying? How many drama shows have adultery, murder, stealing, or malicious gossip at their core? How many sitcoms airing in prime time are filled with sexual innuendo and immorality?

I don't want to live according to the world's standards. The Word of God calls me to a higher, better, more peaceful way of living that truly gives me hope, a steady awareness of God's presence and love, and a desire to live up to my faith potential.

When I don't have a good answer to a question or problem in my life, the Word of God calls me to seek out *godly* counselors. The Bible says,

- "Where there is no counsel, the people fall;
  But in the multitude of counselors there is safety."
  (Proverbs 11:14)
- "Deceit is in the heart of those who devise evil,
  But counselors of peace have joy." (Proverbs 12:20)

- "Without counsel, plans go awry,

  But in the multitude of counselors they are
  established." (Proverbs 15:22)

Seek Out God's Answers! There was a time when I was working with Doc Ebonee that I thought, "Is this ever going to change? I'm doing the things that I believe are right to do, with the right attitude and relationship with this horse, but I'm just not seeing any progress." Yes, there were days when I was discouraged.

At times, I felt impressed that I simply needed to *continue* to do what I knew was right to do.

At other times, I felt that it might be a good idea to seek out the counsel of experts, and to say, "Watch what I'm doing and tell me if you see that I should change something."

In our spiritual walk, there are times when it can be a very good thing to ask someone:

How do I experience more of God?

How do I get more out of the Word of God?

How do I develop the patience to wait on God's timing?

How do I know when I should forge ahead, and when I should be quiet and try to listen more clearly to what God is telling me?

These all are very good questions that can produce good results, if we will do what the wise counselor advises us. The key, however, is to ask these questions FIRST of the Holy Spirit, and to look for our answers FIRST in the Word of God.

The Word of God Sets Up New
Opportunities for Ministry

The Word of God creates a mindset in me that is always looking for the next "move" God wants me to make. That move might be a decision I am to make, an appointment I am to schedule, or perhaps a telephone call I am to make. Nearly always, the moves that God leads me to make are moves that will help me to be a better pastor or to preach a better sermon.

Even if you aren't a pastor, let me assure you, the next moves God will lead you to make will be moves that will help you be both a better person, and be more successful in whatever line of work God has called you to pursue.

Let me explain further.

As a minister, who generally has a sermon that must be preached on a Sunday morning, I find that much of my "think time" becomes focused on what the Lord might want me to say the coming Sunday. I once read that it takes an hour to ninety minutes of preparation time—thinking, praying, reading, studying, making notes or writing out ideas, looking up Scriptures, doing research—for every minute that is spent actually delivering a top-notch sermon.

As an ADHD person, I couldn't begin to set aside two ten-hour preparation sessions for a twenty-minute sermon! But, because of the way I learn and because of my bent toward applying or acting on everything the Lord brings to my mind from the Word of God, I find that I am virtually preparing *all the time* for what's going to happen on the following Sunday morning. Much of my research takes place as I listen to the Holy Spirit, act on what He says, and contemplate the results.

For example, if the Lord brings a person's name or image to my mind, my first response is to pray for that person. I may not know anything that is going on in that person's life, but if their name or face comes to mind, I probably know enough about the person to know *something* to pray.

If the person's name or face *continues* to come to mind, I pick up the phone and call that person. Inevitably, that opens up a conversation that nearly always has an opportunity for me to minister to the person in some way, speaking God's Word into their life in relationship to a need the person has voiced, a problem the person is experiencing, or a decision the person is facing. Nearly always I have an added opportunity to pray for the person before we end the call.

Without breaking any confidences or divulging private information, that episode in my life, and that conversation, might become part of a larger issue related to Christian living that the Lord wants me to address in a sermon. I can reflect back on the phone call and ask,

Which Scriptures did the Lord bring to mind to help this person?

How did the Holy Spirit lead me to pray for the person?

What words of wisdom or counsel did the Lord lead me to give to the person?

And what were the results, or what are LIKELY to be the results in the aftermath of the call?

If you are not a minister, but let's say, a salesman, you may find yourself asking,

What words of wisdom did the Lord bring to mind to help that client?

How did the Holy Spirit lead me to talk with or pray with the person?

What are the eternal results that might come as the result of our conversation?

If you approach *every* encounter as being "God arranged," then even if you don't make a sale, you can have tremendous satisfaction and feelings of fulfillment at the end of the day that you have done something truly beneficial in God's eyes!

I've heard pastors say that they struggle from time to time with WHAT to preach on a Sunday morning. I tend to have the exact opposite problem. There are too many topics that I believe are important to address. I rarely if ever have too little to say. The problem is usually that I have too much to say and people have too little inclination to stay in church for several hours to hear it all!

Just recently as I spoke this Word aloud, the Lord directed me to a passage in the Old Testament that described the actions of a king of Israel. I saw clearly, with insight I had never had before, that this king always seemed to be coming back to God as a "last resort" after he had tried other things first—things that counselors and family members had suggested to him. I had a new understanding that I need to go to God *first* with *everything*—every decision, every choice, and every response. I need to get God's guidance before I seek the counsel or opinions of any other person. Rather than have God's Word confirm what others tell me, I need to have God's Word firmly in my mind and heart and then, see if the words of others confirm that to me.

I asked someone close to me, "What does this verse about seeking FIRST the kingdom of God mean to you?" That person's response was, "It means that I cannot or must not *expect* God to meet all my needs if I don't trust Him first."

Yet another person said to me, "It means that when I seek the kingdom of God first, my sense of need is likely to change and I will see more clearly that God has always and will always meet my real *needs.*"

These were two very different applications of this verse from my own application. Each of them is entirely valid and valuable. Each of them is very personal. And I suspect that in the future, when this verse from the Word of God is spoken, we three will each have even more insight into what it means to seek God's kingdom FIRST.

The Word of God in our uniquely designed mouths functioned to give us unique direction. As we three shared what God had revealed to us, we each gained further "revelation knowledge." What a manifestation of God's amazing design to have His absolute, unchanging, and universal Word produce highly individualized application! And what an example of how the BODY of Christ is intended to function.

The Word of God
Changes Our Thinking

The Bible calls us to experience a "renewal" of our mind—that means a change in the way we *think*.

A number of years ago, the Lord impressed upon me these three statements:

- If you keep on thinking the way you have always thought, you will always get what you have always been thinking.

- If you keep on seeing the way you've always seen, you will always get what you have always been seeing.

- If you keep on speaking the way you've always spoken, you will always get what you have always been speaking.

God's plan for us is ongoing, continual renewal—growing into a fresh *new* way of thinking, seeing, and speaking.

All of us are subject to ongoing and continual *retraining*. We can learn new ways. We can learn to think, see, and speak the way God does! We can receive new things in our lives that are the things God desires for us to have, but which we have not yet received because we have been so intent on thinking, seeing, and speaking in our old ways.

The more I read and apply the Word of God to my life, the more I find myself thinking the Word. The more I *think* the Word, the quicker I am to speak the Word. And the quicker I am to speak the Word, the more likely it is that I will actually ACT on the Word.

When I truly think, see, speak, and act on the Word of God, I become more useful to the Lord on this earth. Those who are used by God to help others are those who truly *thrive* in this life, not merely survive.

Of Greater Use to God. Let me return to the way this chapter started—with a reminder of what a "bit" does, and how it relates to the other parts of a bridle.

The bit is connected to a "headstall," a strip of leather that goes over the head that keeps the bit in the horse's mouth. The bit is also connected to the reins that are held in the rider's hands. Taken together, the headstall, bit, and reins are the "bridle."

One day when I was in our tack room looking at various bridles, I had an immediate awareness that the bridle is a great metaphor for the Trinity.

God the Father is the One who is our head. He is the One who created us according to His wonderful plan and purpose, instilling in us all of the specific talents and abilities that we would need to fulfill His purpose. He is the One who sent the Word to create everything in the universe. He is the One who authorized Jesus to be the living Word on this earth. (See John 1:1–2.)

Jesus, as the Word, used words to heal, to deliver, and to set people free. God's Word in our mouths must always be in alignment with what Jesus said, including the Old Testament and other New Testament writers that either give preface to or give follow-up teaching of what Jesus said. The Word of God is intended to be for our benefit, and for us to be of benefit to others around us. The Word of God is never intended to injure, destroy, or to diminish a person's faith—rather, to create, build up, and encourage!

The Holy Spirit is the Person of the Trinity who has been given authority to lead us and guide us. He shows us how to apply the Word of God. He reminds us of what Jesus said and what the Bible teaches. He puts together various passages of the Word to reveal new insights and levels of understanding. He directs us to where, when, and how we should give voice to the Word of God for maximum benefit, to ourselves and to others.

We must acknowledge at all times that we are God's creation, made for God's pleasure and plans. We must acknowledge that Jesus is our Savior, inspiring us to speak as He spoke and do what He did. We must acknowledge that the Holy Spirit leads us to follow the footsteps of Jesus as our Lord, going where and doing what God desires in any given day or season of our lives.

Take a horse's bridle off and that horse will do what it wants to do, without any regard to other horses or people.

Take the divine bridle off our lives and we are left to our own devices, lusts, and ideas about what is right and wrong.

Put a horse's bridle ON and it becomes subject to its rider and is *useful*, whether simply for riding pleasure or for winning a world championship.

Put the divine bridle on our lives and we become useful to the Lord in ways that bring us personal fulfillment and joy, and also for the spreading of the Gospel and the building up of God's people.

Our choice must be, "Put Your bridle on me, God!"

I encourage you to make that your prayer today . . . and for the rest of your life!

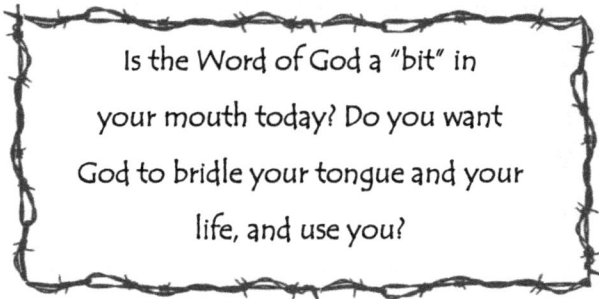

Is the Word of God a "bit" in your mouth today? Do you want God to bridle your tongue and your life, and use you?

11

LEARNING TO LISTEN AND LISTENING TO LEARN

Much of the way a child learns is by asking questions. Children often ask, "What's that? What's that *for*?" They ask, "How do I do that?" They ask, "How many days until Christmas?" They want to know, "Are we almost there?"

Questions are also the way most of us learn *how* to follow Jesus as Lord. We are wise to go to God's Word with the question, "How should I live today, Lord, in a way that will be pleasing to You, purposeful, and in keeping with the potential You have put in me?"

There are many analogies and metaphors that the Lord has given me in my experiences with horses . . . for helping people walk out their Christian life. In this chapter,

I'm going to give you six of these. Each is presented in the form of a question, with an application based on God's Word.

I invite you to use these if you need to present a devotional word to a group in your church, or as the beginning point for a Bible study or Bible-based conversation. Even if you do not share these messages with others, God can use them in your life as you read and reflect on them.

Key Question #1:
Are You Learning What You Need to Know
to Grow in Your Relationship with Christ Jesus?

In the world of show horses, there are three things that every horse must be *trained* to do. These things are not instinctual. They must be taught and learned.

First, every horse needs to learn how to walk STRAIGHT. A horse's natural tendency is to meander and to walk in large curves. If you go out to a pasture and look at the natural trails the horses create, you'll find that they are not straight-line paths. They have many curves.

As followers of the Lord, we need to learn God's commands for how to walk a straight path before Him—

a walk that is an application of God's commandments and a walk that demonstrates that we have heard and are heeding the Holy Spirit's guidance. We may long to *run,* to do great exploits for the Lord, but first we need to learn how to *walk* out God's lifestyle for us—day by day, month by month, year by year, situation after situation, in all of life's relationships and circumstances.

God's Word says, "Strengthen the hands which hang down, and the feeble knees, and make straight paths for your feet, so that what is lame may not be dislocated, but rather be healed." (See Hebrews 12:12–13.)

Second, every horse needs to learn to quiet its mind so that it is open to a trainer's signals. A quiet horse is a horse that has expended all of its extra mental energy, and is focused and ready to receive training instruction.

The Lord speaks to us when we come to a position of resting before Him. *Resting* was not an easy thing for me to do initially. I have a very active mind—in fact, my mind usually seems to be racing at more than a hundred miles an hour. I am easily distracted and very creative, and have a lot of mental energy. I have learned, however, that there is tremendous benefit in *quieting my mind* so I can hear from the Lord clearly. He is always speaking. I must develop my whole being so I am always listening.

God's Word says, "Be still and know that I am God." (See Psalm 46:10.)

Third, every horse is subject to a SEQUENCE in its training. A horse needs to learn how to *walk* in the way its rider directs. There's no point in getting a horse to trot—which is a faster pace—if it doesn't first yield to the rider's commands at a walk.

It is only after a horse has mastered the trot that it is ready to lope (a term that indicates a slow gallop but certainly not a full run).

I believe that most followers of the Lord struggle at times with wanting God to be on *their* timetable, rather than for them to be on the Lord's timetable. We often want more responsibility, and greater opportunities for ministry, and a high level of blessings, *before* we are ready to handle those responsibilities and opportunities, or use great blessings wisely.

God knows when we are ready for "more" and He is always patient with us, and at the same time, more than willing to give us more when we are ready to handle it.

God is never in a hurry. Most of us need to slow down in order to become quiet before the Lord and learn what God has for us to learn and apply.

We need to learn to pray as the psalmist prayed, "Direct my steps by Your word, and let no iniquity have dominion over me." (Psalm 119:133)

Key Question #2:

How Are *YOU* Responding to

Life's Anxieties and Frustrations?

When most people experience frustrations or "worries," they do one of two things—they attempt to flee, or they stand their ground and fight. How do you decide?

First, you need to consider your "defensive" weapons.

Horses can bite, kick, and run. That's pretty much the extent of their defensive "weaponry." A mare will generally stand her ground and protect her colt if it is in danger, even to the point of sacrificing her life. But, she has little means of defense other than biting and kicking. If a horse is on its own with NO colt to protect, it usually will attempt to outrun an enemy.

The Bible tells us that we can put on the whole armor of God as our defense against evil—against the devil and all those he inspires to do evil. Ephesians 6:11–18 tells us that we must

- gird ourselves with truth (develop the mindset that Truth is the reality of God's Word being inspired for our benefit)

- put on a breastplate of righteousness (we are to be in a relationship with God through Jesus Christ as our Savior)

- shod our feet with the preparation of the gospel of peace (so we might go where we go with the message of God's grace so that others might be saved)
- put on the helmet of salvation (putting God's Word in our mind to protect our mind from the influence of all that comes at us from the world that is NOT in alignment with God's Word)
- pick up the shield of faith (believing God is committed to do what God's Word says)

The only weapon used for offense provided by the apostle Paul in this passage is the sword of the Spirit, which he says is the "WORD OF GOD"! Paul describes the Word of God as *powerful*.

And then, once we are fully armed—which is a grand metaphor for putting on Christ from head to toe—we are to do one thing: PRAY!

Second, you need to look around and see who is nearby and on your side.

Horses have a strong herd instinct. In any given herd, there is usually a dominant stallion and a dominant mare, especially when horses run the open range. Even in a more controlled environment, horses like to be with other horses and they develop bonds that we might interpret in human terms as "friendships." If you keep two horses in adjacent stalls in a barn over a length of time, and then you remove one of those horses from the barn, you are likely to find that the remaining horse exhibits increased anxiety. It seems that the horse is aware that his "buddy" has been taken away, and that upsets the environmental equilibrium for that animal.

If given a choice in an open pasture, horses will tend to group themselves together and move together naturally. This perhaps is a holdover from days when horses found safety in a herd from predators, but even in the modern pasture, there is a pattern that indicates horses truly *like* being with other horses.

God's Word tells us that we are to stay in fellowship with other believers. We are to pray in agreement with other believers, and seek God's presence in our midst any time two or more of us are gathered together.

Third, you need to ask whether you are feeling anxious about something that is an absolute command or truth in God's Word, or something that is a matter of personal style or preference.

Horses can exhibit very different responses to similar situations. For example, not all horses love to perform or even to follow prescribed routines of behavior. You can see in some horses' eyes and in the way they hold themselves that they are choosing to be obedient, but they aren't having any fun. They are going to do what the trainer asks them to do, but without much expression or enthusiasm.

Part of the reason for this is that horses are too often kept in stalls for too long a time. A horse would much rather be free to roam an open pasture! This is true for human beings, too. I doubt if there are any prisoners who truly *enjoy* being in a prison cell. For that matter, many people who work in office cubicles or have a tightly controlled or small workspace on a factory line are likely NOT to delight in the "space" they occupy hour after hour. Children often find a classroom desk a very confining space—they can hardly wait for the bell to ring so they can escape to the nearest playground.

We each must discover our own likes and dislikes, our own preferences, and our own "style" when it comes to learning, designing our environments, and making personal choices about what to wear and how to fix our hair. We each also must take a look at our own schedule and routines and determine if we are factoring enough relaxation and good clean "fun" into our life.

Horses show stress. They can develop ulcers related to anxiety.

Horses are subject to boredom. If given a choice between being with other horses in a pasture or standing in a stall waiting for the next training session, a horse will choose time in the pasture *every time*!

God wants us to be productive, but He also wants us to relax in His presence and enjoy "just being" with Him.

God's Word tells us, "Be anxious for nothing, but in everything by prayer and supplication [asking with intense desire], with thanksgiving, let your requests be made known to God; and the peace of God, which surpasses all understanding, will guard your hearts and minds through Christ Jesus." (Philippians 4:6–7)

Key Question #3:
How Are You Handling Your Fears?

Horses are smart in ways that many people are not. They have very strong instincts and sensory abilities that enable them to "read" people with great accuracy.

Horses can "smell" fear. When a person is afraid, that person's body puts off an aroma that is subtle but nevertheless, real and penetrating. Even if a person has sprayed himself with all kinds of scents—from toothpaste and mouthwash to hair gels, deodorants, and colognes—a horse is able to smell fear in the person.

Horses also can read body language with tremendous accuracy. A horse can tell by the way a person moves, and the edge in a person's voice, that a person is filled with fear. It doesn't take long for a horse to read the facial features, manner of walking, posture, or voice patterns.

Horses are generally afraid to go into shadows, or through water. That's largely owing to the fact that horses have no depth perception. They don't know how "deep" a shadow may be. They cannot gauge how deep a body of water might be. If it is within their leap span, a horse usually will choose to leap over a shadow or water.

A horse will take the risk of moving into a shadow or going into water for one of two reasons, in my opinion. A horse can be beaten into submission—in other words, *forced* into a shadow or stream. Or, a horse can follow the desire of its rider because it has come to *trust* the rider not to lead it into a dangerous or troubling situation.

The truth is that none of us knows the depth of a trouble that we encounter. Neither do we have the ability to see the full consequences of any circumstance or difficulty we encounter in life. Sometimes we think a trouble is "small" and it opens up with such gaping jaws that we scramble for our lives. At other times, we may think of a trouble as very large, but as we enter it, we discover that it is mostly illusion and very little substance and we are able to find a way over, through, around, or under the trouble to the other side of it.

And an equal truth is that none of us knows the full depth and power of God's Word! None of us truly knows the full ramifications of God's Word *applied with faith!*

What the Word of God calls us to do is to follow Jesus as our Lord until we come to the place where we trust God to lead us in such a way that a trouble will *not* overwhelm us or rob us of eternal life in Christ Jesus. We come to the place where we can declare, "I can do all things through Christ." (See Philippians 4:13.)

When we are willing to trust God and to act as He directs us, we find that we have a boldness or courage that is beyond our natural instinct. We develop a strong foundation of faith that we are going to walk through circumstances that might otherwise be very frightening to us, and not only *survive* the negative situation, but *thrive.*

Trusting God's Word is required, and especially *trusting* God's Word to hold true when times are difficult. Proverbs 3:5–6 says, "Trust in the LORD with all your heart, and lean not on your own understanding; in all your ways acknowledge Him, and He will direct your paths."

Key Question #4:
How Shiny Is Your Coat?

The ideal for the *show ring* is for a horse to be "slick"—to have short hair that shines.

Many people believe that a horse's coat becomes shiny through brushing. That is partly true, but let me assure you, if a horse's hair is long, you can brush that horse vigorously and consistently, and the horse will not shed its long hair until its body has concluded that it doesn't need or isn't going to need added thickness of hair to keep it warm.

The length and thickness of a horse's hair is nearly always determined by the amount of daylight the horse receives through its "eye gate."

For example, the summer solstice toward the end of June is the longest day of the year—where I live in Kansas, we have about sixteen hours of daylight on that day. That amount of daylight sends a message to a horse that it doesn't *need* to have a thick coat of hair to stay warm. Rather, it will be to the horse's advantage and comfort level to have less and shorter hair.

As the months of summer pass and the autumn season kicks in, the horse intuitively senses that winter is coming. There's a little less light every day, something that is pretty much imperceptible to human beings on a day-to-day basis. The horse, however, sees less daylight as a signal that it needs to grow more hair. He needs to get himself prepared for cold days and nights!

A person who keeps a show horse in a barn generally puts blankets and hoods on the horse to keep it from being chilled, and puts a timer on the barn lights. The timer is set to stay on for sixteen hours, keeping the horse's system a little "tricked."

When a horse has short hair, more of the oil from the horse's skin can be worked into the hair with brushing, making the coat of the horse more beautiful. It also allows for the horse's coat to be cleaned more readily, and to harbor less and less dirt and other pollutants.

Can you see the spiritual analogy?

The Word of God states repeatedly that it is not good for men and women to live in "darkness." That means living in a state where there is a *lack* of information or a *lack* of information being properly applied. Jesus referred to Himself as the "Light," and He also referred to those who followed Him closely as people who were "light" in their world.

Further, the Word of God tells us the Scriptures have been given to us by God to be a "lamp unto our feet" and a "light unto our path." (See Psalm 119:105.) Both the word *lamp* and the word *light* in that passage refer to knowledge. God's Word shows us our next step in life—it gives us guidance for today's decisions, today's choices, today's agenda. God's Word also shows us the direction in which we are to walk—it gives us guidance about the goals that are right for us to pursue. This knowledge is very specific—it is knowledge for us *personally.*

God's Word is the knowledge about how I am to live, and if I live the way God intends, He can be trusted to use my life as a model or pattern for others. I don't need to club anybody over the head with the truth that God is good to have in one's life, or that Jesus is the Savior. God will use the words and deeds of my life to draw people to ask, "What's your secret?"

On the other hand, if the Word of God is not real to you, and you aren't living it out in practical ways, how can the Word become real to others who observe your life?

Until a person truly trusts Jesus to be the Light, and to trust the Word of God to be the source of all the knowledge that is necessary to live a good and noble life, that person isn't likely to "let go" of the things that are holding the person back from all of God's blessings and rewards, or making a full commitment to living God's way.

The parallel between the natural and spiritual is very strong in this case. When we are people who live with a strong awareness of and influence from the Light, we are going to let more of the oil of the Holy Spirit surface in us and impact all things in our natural life. We are going to attract and harbor fewer pollutants and the "filth" of this world. We are going to present a brighter countenance and a more positive life to others around us.

The Word of God states that people perish because they are walking in darkness, not fully understanding or applying the truth of God. Our challenge as those who are trusting Jesus as Lord is to stay as close to His light as we can stay! We are to walk in the light, live in the light, and be a reflection of His light!

Key Question #5:
Does Change Upset You?

Are you aware that there is a different foot pattern used by horses, depending on how fast the horse is moving?

A walk is a four-beat gait. Each foot is going to hit the ground at different times, in a one-two-three-four sequence.

A trot is a two-beat gait. Two feet are hitting at the same time—the right front and back left, or the left front and back right.

A lope is a three-beat gait. The right rear leg, for example, propels the horse forward. On the next beat the horse catches itself on the left rear and right front legs while the other hind leg is still momentarily on the ground. On the third beat, the horse catches itself on the left front leg while the diagonal pair is momentarily still in contact with the ground.

The left front leg is extended more and is matched by a slightly more extended hind leg on the same side. This is referred to as a "lead." It is desirable for a horse to lead with its inside legs when on a circle. Therefore, a horse that begins cantering with the right rear leg as described above will have the left front and hind legs each land farther forward. This would be referred to as being on the "left lead."

At the horse show in the trail class the obstacles are arranged in a sequence that requires a horse to *enter* each obstacle or pattern on a precise foot in order to move smoothly through the obstacle without any hesitation. In the Western Riding and Reining classes the horse is required to change leads. Throughout the pattern the horse will change from his left to right lead and then from his right to left lead.

A rider and horse can adjust the horse's lead foot with a little "hop" or something like a stutter step or skip. But the best performances are ones in which the switching of lead feet is so smooth and seamless that the change is virtually imperceptible. This takes a great deal of time to develop, and requires a very keen understanding of the horse's individual gait and ways of moving.

In our walk with the Lord, we each face a wide variety of obstacles and new situations. The Lord knows *how* we are made. He knows *how* we can move successfully through the circumstances of our life with the least upheaval and least emotional struggle. Furthermore, the Lord knows our faith level and, above all, He knows what He desires to teach us as He walks with us *through* difficult situations.

One of the major signs of a mature Christian is the ability to be so in tune with the Holy Spirit, and so sensitive to His directives, that we adjust our approach to problems, and our actions within difficult relationships and situations, to be in complete accord with the Spirit's *leading.* We must come to the place where we are moving spiritually in total sync with His desires, plans, and purposes. We are quiet in our spirits. We have no jagged or abrupt behaviors—rather, we are in the "flow" that He has designed for us.

This doesn't happen quickly or easily. It is the result of a great deal of time and increased sensitivity to *how* we listen to the Lord and *how* we trust Him in all things. It is a result of our applying God's Word in hundreds of ways in hundreds of circumstances.

God's Word encourages us that the Lord wants us to "be filled with the knowledge of His will in all wisdom and spiritual understanding; that you may walk worthy of the Lord, fully pleasing Him, being fruitful in every good work and increasing in the knowledge of God." (See Colossians 1:9–10.) Our goal must be to develop such a close relationship with the Holy Spirit that change does not upset us! We can walk with confidence that God is leading us through every problem and difficult circumstance . . . with victory just ahead!

Key Question #6:
Are You Getting All of
Your Needs Met?

There are five things that every horse needs. People need these very same things:

1. Good Nutrition. Our nutrition as followers of Christ Jesus is the Word of God—reading it, studying it, and hearing it. We must take in God's Word on a regular basis, and for me, that definitely means a "daily feeding" of God's Word.

When it comes to nutrition, there are nearly always "deficiencies" of vitamins and minerals at some time, and to some degree. In the horse world, added supplements are put in the horse's feed. For us, there are times when we are faced with a particular problem, and we need to go to God's Word with a concordance in hand and study specific passages that can give us specific answers. At other times, we become aware of issues in our life—or are reminded or "plagued" by issues from our childhood or earlier years— that also need to be addressed in very specific ways.

If we fail to take in the truth, we inevitably will buy into a lie. The lies are presented all around us, in countless ways—through people we meet, temptations we feel, and the messages of the media. We cannot avoid lies. What we can do is refuse to let those lodge in our minds and hearts. As a man once said, "I can't keep the birds from flying over my head, but I can keep them from nesting in my hair." The only antidote for lies is a good dose of the truth, and the purest form of truth on this earth is your direct consumption of the Word of God.

2. Good Rest. Rest in most cases goes beyond sleep and recreation. We must learn to "quiet" our spirits and minds. We must spend time in contemplation or meditation on God's Word—taking time to think about things, praying quietly about things, considering what we have read in light of experiences in our past or circumstances in our present. The more we read and *memorize* God's Word, the more we have ready access to "digest" God's Word in any place, at any time. We can learn to rest in short spurts, but there is tremendous benefit in taking time periodically for breaks where we can read and then meditate on God's Word for longer stretches of time—hours, and even an entire afternoon or day.

3. Good Training Exercise. God's Word challenges us, but sometimes that challenge can take on the form of

153

going to a particular conference, participating in a regular Bible study group, taking a course at church or at a Bible training institute, or listening to an entire audible teaching series. These are the types of "exercise" that build upon what we already know in God's Word, and "stretch" us with new ideas and insights.

The ultimate exercise, of course, is our active application of what we read. Every day is a training day with the Lord. The Holy Spirit has a way of putting us through *His* paces to teach us by example. We each face different opportunities every day to do the *work* of the Gospel—giving a specific word or blessing to a person or group, modeling the life of Christ in a difficult situation, or going to a person in need and praying for that person.

4. Consistency and Endurance. The Christian life is nearly always evaluated on the criterion of *consistency*—over time. Our following the Lord isn't a one-time decision or an event that gives us a spiritual "high," a phenomenal miracle, or the opportunity to hear (or preach) a superstar-quality sermon that makes a great difference, either in your life or the life of another person. It is the daily walking out of the life of Christ on this earth.

It isn't going to church once or twice a year. It is going every week.

It isn't starting a Bible study by going to the first or second session. It is attending regularly and completing that Bible study.

It isn't reading your Bible for a few minutes once a month. It is reading your Bible daily.

It isn't thanking and praising God when a major blessing appears in your life. It is thanking and praising God in an almost nonstop way for whatever He sends your way.

5. Good Therapeutic Care. We tend to know when we are sick enough in body to need a doctor. We need to recognize that God has raised up counselors and therapists to help us in a wide variety of ways that are related to emotional, psychological, or spiritual conditions. If your marriage is in trouble, get help. If you are feeling depressed, get help. If you are struggling with a particular spiritual issue—don't walk away from the church or the Lord, walk toward the Lord and seek out someone who can help you through wise words and prayer.

Horses need our *care*. They can't stay at the peak of their performance without human help. We also need care. We need to take care of ourselves, and we need to thank the Lord continually for being the ultimate source of our care.

God's Word tells us that God loves us with a depth of love we cannot even imagine. When we hurt, God alone knows how to heal us *completely* and for all eternity. The

Word says, "Humble yourselves under the mighty hand of God, that He may exalt you in due time, casting all your care upon Him, for *He cares for you*." (See 1 Peter 5:6–7.) Never forget it!

To Learn More . . .

To learn more about Tim O'Neal Ministries, to invite Tim or Gypsy to speak, or to find out more information about their books and DVDs, write:

Tim O'Neal Ministries

P.O. Box 749

Fort Scott, Kansas 66701

Or, check out their website! There is room for you to communicate with the O'Neals on the website:

www.timonealministries.com

www.ingramcontent.com/pod-product-compliance
Lightning Source LLC
Chambersburg PA
CBHW071451070426
42452CB00039B/1030